First World War
and Army of Occupation
War Diary
France, Belgium and Germany

60 DIVISION
Divisional Troops
Royal Army Medical Corps
2/6 London Field Ambulance
18 September 1915 - 27 November 1916

WO95/3029/5

The Naval & Military Press Ltd
www.nmarchive.com
Published in association with The National Archives

Published by

The Naval & Military Press Ltd

Unit 10 Ridgewood Industrial Park,

Uckfield, East Sussex,

TN22 5QE England

Tel: +44 (0) 1825 749494

www.naval-military-press.com

www.nmarchive.com

This diary has been reprinted in facsimile from the original. Any imperfections are inevitably reproduced and the quality may fall short of modern type and cartographic standards.

© Crown Copyright
Images reproduced by permission of The National Archives, London, England, 2015.

Contents

Document type	Place/Title	Date From	Date To
Heading	WO95/3029/4		
Heading	60th Division 2-6th London Fld Amb. 1915 Aug-1916 Nov		
Miscellaneous	Summary August 1915		
Miscellaneous	2/6th London Field Ambulance		
War Diary	Bishops Stortford	18/09/1915	25/09/1915
Miscellaneous	From O.C. Has Field Ambulance To H.D. His 60 Lous Div. T.F.	02/11/1915	02/11/1915
War Diary	Bishops Stortford	01/10/1918	30/10/1918
Miscellaneous	From O.C. 2/6 Found Field Ambulance		
War Diary	Hockeril	01/11/1915	04/11/1915
War Diary	Bocking	05/11/1915	29/11/1915
Heading	War Diary of the 2/6th London Field Ambulance From 1st December 1915 To 31st December 1915 Volume 12		
War Diary	Braintree	02/12/1915	20/12/1915
Miscellaneous	2/6th London Field Ambulance Operation Orders	30/12/1915	30/12/1915
Miscellaneous	181st Infantry Brigade Brigade Exercise December 2nd	29/11/1915	29/11/1915
Operation(al) Order(s)	181st Brigade Order No.2	20/12/1915	20/12/1915
Operation(al) Order(s)	181st Infantry Brigade Order No. 1		
Miscellaneous	Appendix I		
Miscellaneous	Notes.		
Miscellaneous	General Idea		
Operation(al) Order(s)	181st Infantry Brigade Order No.1	29/12/1915	29/12/1915
Operation(al) Order(s)	181st Infantry Brigade Order No.2	30/12/1915	30/12/1915
Miscellaneous	2/6th London Field Ambulance Operation Order For December 30th 1915	30/12/1915	30/12/1915
Heading	War Diary March 1st To March 31st 1916 2/6th London Field Ambulance		
War Diary	Sutton Veny	01/03/1916	31/03/1916
Miscellaneous	Programme of Training 2/6th. London Field Ambulance		
Miscellaneous	Programme of Training for Week Ending 18th March 1918		
Heading	War Diary April 1st To April 30th 1916 2/6th London Field Ambulance		
Miscellaneous	Programme of Training 2/6 London Field Ambulance Week Ending	29/04/1916	29/04/1916
Miscellaneous	Appendix D		
Miscellaneous	Programme of Traning 2/6th London Field Ambulance		
Miscellaneous	Appendix A		
War Diary	Sutton Veny	01/04/1916	30/04/1916
Heading	War Diary May 1st To May 31st 1916 2/6th London Field Ambulance		
Miscellaneous	Programme of Traning 2/6th London Field Training Week End May 6th 1916		
Miscellaneous	Programme of Traning For Week Ending 13th May 1916 2/6th London Field Ambulance		
Miscellaneous	Programme of Training for Week Ending 20th May 2/6th London Field Ambulance		
Miscellaneous	Programme of Traning Week Ending May 27th 1916	20/05/1916	20/05/1916

Type	Description	Start	End
Miscellaneous	Programme of Traning To May 30th 2/6th London Ambulance		
War Diary	Sutton Veny	01/05/1916	31/05/1916
Heading	War Diary June 1st To June 22nd 1916 2/6th London Field Ambulance.		
Miscellaneous	2/6th London Field Ambulance Programme Of Training For Weekending	03/06/1916	03/06/1916
Miscellaneous	Appendix "A"		
Miscellaneous	Programme of Training 2/6th London Ambulance	10/06/1916	10/06/1916
Miscellaneous	Appendix "C"		
Miscellaneous	Programme of Training 2/6th London Field Ambulance Week Ending	09/06/1916	09/06/1916
Miscellaneous	Appendix "B"		
Miscellaneous	Instructions Re Division Proceeding Overseas	24/06/1916	24/06/1916
Miscellaneous	Appendix "D"		
Miscellaneous	Programme of Training 2/6th London Field Ambulance Week Ending	10/06/1916	10/06/1916
Heading	War Diary of 2/6th London Field Ambulance From 23rd June 1916 To 30th July 1916		
War Diary	Warminster	23/06/1916	23/06/1916
War Diary	Southampton	23/06/1916	23/06/1916
War Diary	Le Havre	24/06/1916	25/06/1916
War Diary	St. Pol	26/06/1916	26/06/1916
War Diary	Neuviele Au Cornet	27/06/1916	27/06/1916
War Diary	Guestreville	28/06/1916	01/07/1916
War Diary	Mingoval	02/07/1916	13/07/1916
War Diary	Haute Avesnes	13/07/1916	29/07/1916
Heading	War Diary of 2/6th London Field Ambulance From 1st August 1916 To 31st August 1916		
War Diary	Haute Avesnes	01/08/1916	12/08/1916
War Diary	Anzin	12/08/1916	12/08/1916
War Diary	Haute Avesnes	11/08/1916	20/08/1916
War Diary	Aux Rietz	20/08/1916	20/08/1916
War Diary	Haute Avesnes	21/08/1916	30/08/1916
War Diary	Sutton Veny	01/06/1916	22/06/1916
Heading	War Diary of 2/6th London Field Ambulance From 1st September 1916 To 30th September 1916		
War Diary	Haute Avesnes	01/09/1916	28/09/1916
Heading	60th Div 2/6 London F Amb Oct 1916		
Heading	War Diary of the 2/6 London Field Ambulance From October 1st 1916 To October 31st 1916		
War Diary	Haute Avesnes	01/10/1916	23/10/1916
War Diary	Anzin	23/10/1916	23/10/1916
War Diary	Haute Avesnes	23/10/1916	24/10/1916
War Diary	Sus-St-Leger	24/10/1916	28/10/1916
War Diary	Neuvillette	29/10/1916	29/10/1916
War Diary	Monplaisir	29/10/1916	30/10/1916
Heading	War Diary of 2/6th London Field Ambulance From November 1st 1916 To November 30th 1916		
War Diary	Mon Plaisir	01/11/1916	02/11/1916
War Diary	Mon Plaisir-Gorges	03/11/1916	03/11/1916
War Diary	Gorges Vauchelles-Les-Domart	04/11/1916	04/11/1916
War Diary	Vauchelles-Les-Domart	06/11/1916	15/11/1916
War Diary	Vauchelles-L-Domt (Bellancourt)	16/11/1916	17/11/1916
War Diary	Vauchelles-L-Domt	18/09/1916	24/09/1916
War Diary	Marseilles	27/11/1916	27/11/1916

WO 95/3029/4

60TH DIVISION

2-6TH LONDON FLD AMB.

1915 AUG — 1916 NOV

Summary. August. 1915.

<u>2/6 London Field Ambulance</u>. Detailed to 181. Infantry Brigade
60th London Division T.F.
3rd Army.

In Camp at Hocheril. Herts.

Discipline. Has improved since the move under canvas, in part owing to increased supervision and in part to the relief from the monotony of billets for 3 months in a small country town.

Efficiency. Has on the one hand been impaired by the introduction of a large proportion of recruits although they are above the average as a whole in physique & intelligence & on the other hand has been improved by the elimination of the men who had signed for Home Service only.
It is gratifying that a considerable number of men who had originally declined to sign for Foreign Service have now done so. The want of Medical Officers is still a serious handicap to the rapid training of the men.

Preparation for Service Overseas. The same factors have influenced this as the preceding section. More equipment however, has been to hand with which the men are becoming familiar.

The physique of the men is improving & their health has been uniformly good.

Health. As stated above this has been good. No epidemic of infectious disease has occurred.

John M Wells
Major RAMC T
...................................Commanding
2/6th London Field Ambulance.

Ref. O.S. 1st No.29.   COPY No. 7

2/6th London Field Ambulance.

Operation Orders by Aug.27th '15.
by Major J.E.B.Wells, R.A.M.C.,T. Commanding.

Information (1) The Northern Force has been pursuing the enemy defeated at BUNTINGFORD in a S.. direction.
The 181st Infantry Brigade advanced towards HATFIELD HEATH BUT the Southern Force was found to have taken up a strong position S.E. of HATFIELD HEATH and receiving reinforcements counterattacked forcing the main body of the 181st Brigade back toward LITTLE HALLINGBURY.
▼ On receiving news of the intended retreat the 2/6th London Field Ambulance withdrew its stretcher parties and retired toward the Main Dressing Station at BISHOPS STORTFORD leaving the wounded that could not be removed under the protection of the Red Cross Flag of the Geneva Convention.

Intention (2) The 181st Infantry Brigade less the 2/21st Battn. with the 2/6th London Field Ambulance Bearer Sub-Division and 4 men from Tent Subdivision will move from ROOKERILL CAMP at 9.20 a.m.

Starting Point (3) The starting point will be at the North entrance to Warwick Road.

Advance Guard (4) ½ Bearer Sub-Division B Section will accompany
O.C.Capt.Gill Advance Guard, and will be at the starting point at 9.10 a.m.
2/24th Bn.L.R.
2 Coys. & 1
Maxim Gun
2/24th Battn
½ Bearer Sub-
Divn. 2/6th
Lon.Fld.Amb.

Main Body (5) The Head of the Main Body (Order of March in margin)
Hdqrs.Staff will pass the starting point at 9.30.a.m.
2/24th Bn.L.R.
less 2 Coys.
& 1 Maxim Gun
2/23rd Bn.L.R.
2/22nd Bn.L.R.
(less Q Co.)
2/6th Lon.Fld.
Amb. less Tent
Sub- Divn.
½ Bearer Sub-
Divn.

Rear Guard (6) The Rear Guard as per margin will follow 200 yds. in
O.C.Capt. rear of main body.
McComas.
2/22nd Bn.L.R.
Q Coy.2/22nd.
Bn.L.R.

(7) Reports to me at head of Bearer Sub-Divn. A Section 2/6th London Field Ambulance.

Copy No.1. A.D.M.S.   )
     2. Brigade Hdqrs.   )
     3. O.C.Advance Guard) By Cyclist Orderly
     4. O.C.B.Section   )   7.30 a.m.
     5. O.C.C.Section   )   27/8/15.
     6. Orderly Room   )
     7. War Diarys   )

                                     John M Wells
                                     Major R.A.M.C.T.

                                     ....Commanding
                                     2/6th London Field Ambulance.

WAR DIARY
or
INTELLIGENCE SUMMARY.
(Erase heading not required.)

Army Form C. 2118.

Hour, Date, Place	Summary of Events and Information	Remarks and references to Appendices
16.6.15 Bishops Stortford	March to Thidock at Hedgdon Green (4 hrs) Remainder of R. Dublin Fus.).	Weather very hot. Tea & rum promenade & kept moral most except for it's necessary to have ten pins & even delight to check a leak a these plan he has will they been doing (none)

Sin*[illegible]*
[signature] Major [illegible]
O.C. 2/8 dow Feto [illegible]

Army Form C. 2118.

WAR DIARY
or
INTELLIGENCE SUMMARY.
(Erase heading not required.)

Instructions regarding War Diaries and Intelligence Summaries are contained in F.S. Regs., Part II. and the Staff Manual respectively. Title pages will be prepared in manuscript.

Hour, Date, Place	Summary of Events and Information	Remarks and references to Appendices
ASHOPS STORTH		were to close to the [GENERAL STATION?] [railway?] to DUNHAM. The line also to close [tracks?] together. [Urgently?] is [helpfully?] [ordered?] that other [arrangements?] be [promptly?] made.
25.9.16	Lieut. Edward RAWLIFT & 24 N.C.Os & men Seventh Battalion the [North?] [Wilts?] Regt arrived & duties [overlooked?] [rendered?].	[signature]

Oct.

Rochent Camp.
Nov 2ᵈ 1915.

From O.C. 2/6 Lond Field Ambulance
to A.D.M.S. 60 Lond Div. T.F.

Sir, I have the honour to forward herewith
War Diary Summary for last month.
I have not attached the reports sent in for the
Divisional exercise during this period as you
have only lately had & returned them to me.
I have the honour to be,
Sir
Your obedient Servant

John B Wells.
Maj'r R.A.M.C.
....Commanding
2/6th London Field Ambulance.

WAR DIARY
or
INTELLIGENCE SUMMARY.
(Erase heading not required.)

Army Form C. 2118.

Hour, Date, Place	Summary of Events and Information	Remarks and references to Appendices
Oct 1. BISHOPS STORTFORD	Divisional Training. TAKELY — EASTON PARK. under Gen. CALLEY.	Mns.
5	Divisional Exercise (without troops) at BEN EXLEY. The Unit marched to FELSTED, where three to 10 night, and then at BURY FARM. Weather wet.	
6	The Unit marched to BLACK NOTLEY, made main clearing Station at FRIERS FARM + Wagon subsection at CHIPPEL HILL & WHITE NOTLEY. Bivis of Division bivouac at 7 9 P.M. main clearing Station dismounted at 7 P.M. Bivouacs in fields. Weather fine. Field BLACK NOTLEY. weather mainly fine Oct 7 & 8th. Wh slushes	

WAR DIARY
or
INTELLIGENCE SUMMARY.
(Erase heading not required.)

Army Form C. 2118.

Hour, Date, Place	Summary of Events and Information	Remarks and references to Appendices.
Oct 7. BISHOPS STORTFORD	Morning Training (continued).	
6 "	The unit marched back to FELSTEAD. Wells. O-tpee 1st Troop being support, weeds, potatis. Ambulant left first. The unit marched back for FELSTEAD & camp at HOCKERIL.	
12 "	Tactical Exercise. Initial troops away f FARNHAM & MAWDEN. Initial to LINE MADHAM BRENTPELHAM road.	
14 "	To start Exercise (with troops) to new area. Main dressing Station at MIDDLE END. Advanced Dressing Station at FARNHAM GREEN.	[sig]

WAR DIARY
or
INTELLIGENCE SUMMARY.
(Erase heading not required.)

Army Form C. 2118.

Hour, Date, Place	Summary of Events and Information	Remarks and references to Appendices
Delhi 15 October 14	Still everyone in tents — from our house.	
BISHOPS STORTFORD	Mounted Marches with M.I. Infantry Brigade Lefferstead (billets) & Burn Farm for Night.	
20. "	Marches via Younes End to Fratts Green, then on receiving Burial orders sent 2 sect'n divisn to Terling Place for main Body Station & 1 sub divisn to Fuller Street & form Divisnl Collecting Station. Remained Bivving Rather Mr Makee of Faulkbourn. Regn additional waters for Park kourne & Terling where they billetted Anight.	
" 21. "	Marches from Terling via Younes End, Willow	W.J.T.

Army Form C. 2118.

WAR DIARY
or
INTELLIGENCE SUMMARY.
(Erase heading not required.)

Instructions regarding War Diaries and Intelligence Summaries are contained in F.S. Regs., Part II. and the Staff Manual respectively. Title pages will be prepared in manuscript.

Hour, Date, Place	Summary of Events and Information	Remarks and references to Appendices
Mar 21 BISHOPS STORTFORD	2nd CORK GREEN to FELSTEAD where the unit billeted at DUNN FARM & more rich reception room at HICKS GARAGE as before. Moved to camp from FELSTEAD.	
27 "	Inspection of Transport & Horses by the Comdr. Rt.	
28 "	Received by G.O.C. 65th Division & Dismissed.	
29 "	Training & passes week.	
30 "	Capt. S.R. MATTHEWS & tent William & Johns went to BRAINTREE to join demonstration at BOCKING. Revd Scrutton in charge of armed party who left to make great arrangement for the visit	Wes.

(73989) W4141—463. 400,000. 9/14. H.&J.Ltd. Forms/C. 2118/10.

Army Form C. 2118.

WAR DIARY
or
INTELLIGENCE SUMMARY.
(Erase heading not required.)

Instructions regarding War Diaries and Intelligence Summaries are contained in F. S. Regs., Part II. and the Staff Manual respectively. Title pages will be prepared in manuscript.

Hour, Date, Place	Summary of Events and Information	Remarks and references to Appendices
	Unit in billet at BOCKING.	[signature] Major R.A.M.C. Commanding 2/6th London Field Ambulance.

Ramleh
Decr 2. 915.

From O.C.
  2/5 Lond. Field Ambulance

To A.D.M.S.
  60th Lond. Divn. T.F.

Please find War Diary for November 1915. for
this Unit herewith

[signature]
Major R.A.M.C.
Commanding
2/5th London Field Ambulance.

2/6 London Fld Ambulance

Army Form C. 2118.

WAR DIARY
or
INTELLIGENCE SUMMARY.
(Erase heading not required.)

Hour, Date, Place	Summary of Events and Information	Remarks and references to Appendices
Nov 1. 1915. HOCKERIL	Received Notices Nov 1. 1915. Beyond period of Attestn. BOCKING, ESSEX. Capt. L.R.R. McQUEEN i/charge. 2/11 Batt. Lond. Regt. marched to DUNMOW en route for [—] COGGESHALL. Major WELLS reported 2 ambulance turn. a.m.o. a/m.o. DUNMOW. Capt MINETT took over duty as M.O. to evening. Remainder of unit practised bandaging & an evening parade stood + formed —	
" 2. "	Capt. MINETT occasn. turned 2/11 Batt. a M.D.C. COGGESHALL returned to HOCKERIL at night. drivers employed shafor men & transport. Another squad re-engineering.	
" 3. "	Visits to BRAINTREE & toilets WH about area. Unit helping to billet camp.	L.D.W.

WAR DIARY
or
INTELLIGENCE SUMMARY.
(Erase heading not required.)

Army Form C. 2118.

Instructions regarding War Diaries and Intelligence Summaries are contained in F.S. Regs., Part II. and the Staff Manual respectively. Title pages will be prepared in manuscript.

Hour, Date, Place	Summary of Events and Information	Remarks and references to Appendices

November 4. HOCKERILL Unit struck camp & marched via BOCKING via TAKELEY, DUNMOW & BRAINTREE. arriving 5 p.m.

" 5. BOCKING. Lieut M. BROWN R.A.M.C. + 27 NCOs from Division Attachment arrived & addresses for billeting & rations.

Them went & called for their host & furnishing billets, about 40 men & requisitions billets.

Central feeding arranged at HENLEY ASKINS factory. Cooking pans & stove in a cooking field middleton with tent cart kettle.

Men eleven church parade – C/E at BRAINTREE Parish Church.

Army Form C. 2118.

WAR DIARY
or
INTELLIGENCE SUMMARY.
(Erase heading not required.)

Instructions regarding War Diaries and Intelligence Summaries are contained in F.S. Regs., Part II. and the Staff Manual respectively. Title pages will be prepared in manuscript.

Hour, Date, Place	Summary of Events and Information	Remarks and references to Appendices
9 BOCKING	Lieut M BROWN Return'd from Sanitary Detachment Tilb...	
	Unit present. Field training. COSFIELD PARK.	
10 F	" " BOCKING.	
	Lecture by Capt. MINETT (afternoon) & Lecture by (Guide) from Army Issue.	
11	Route March. FISTED.	
12	HEDINGHAM. Fell out of forced march. Paraded Typhoid fever. Church Parade. C. of E. at 9:30. [illeg.] Brigade Chaplain Maj. HOARE –	
	Lieut WEITMORE. Transport officer. Sick 4 days.	
	Leaving after 6 months instruction cadet from [illeg] in Reserve Brigade. per S/2/73 Reg[...]	

WAR DIARY
or
INTELLIGENCE SUMMARY.
(Erase heading not required.)

Army Form C. 2118.

Hour, Date, Place	Summary of Events and Information	Remarks and references to Appendices
16 Sept '15 BOXTELE	(Brigade) Field training (all units) much (bad weather. Rain) heavy fallen & foot flooring	
17	Lieut WETHERED returns from leave. (Brigade) Field trainings cancelled owing to the weather.	
18		
20	O.C. Commandery & Brigade Staff reconnoiter River & through scenes.	
22	Capt MINETT taken over duty as Hospital.	
24	Inspection of Unit by A.D.M.S. 60th DIV T.F. Medical Board on Lieut T.H. Pollard - today to D.A.G. the san pricily Leewarden offrs	/JWW

(73959) W4141—463. 400,000. 9/14. H.&J.Ltd. Forms/C. 2118/10.

Army Form C. 2118.

WAR DIARY
or
INTELLIGENCE SUMMARY.
(Erase heading not required.)

Instructions regarding War Diaries and Intelligence Summaries are contained in F.S. Regs., Part II. and the Staff Manual respectively. Title pages will be prepared in manuscript.

Hour, Date, Place	Summary of Events and Information	Remarks and references to Appendices

Nov 25. K.15 Boreham (March) TWISTED PARK. Bayonet training.

Co. 161 Brigade in the ETR.

26. a false case of cerebro-spinal meningitis occurred
BRAINTREE. 9 men billeted there isolated then ?
Hospital

(West Ty???) Div Sanitary Officer
but used full route march via BRAINTREE
BLACK NOTLEY — RAWDUSH GREEN
BRAINTREE.

[signatures]

C O N F I D E N T I A L.

WAR DIARY of the

2/6th LONDON FIELD AMBULANCE.

From 1st DECEMBER 1915 to 31st DECEMBER 1915.

VOLUME 12.

WAR DIARY
or
INTELLIGENCE SUMMARY.
(Erase heading not required.)

Army Form C. 2118.

Hour, Date, Place	Summary of Events and Information	Remarks and references to Appendices
December 2 BRAMRE 1915	Transport transferred to A.S.C.	
" 3rd	Repair training ABBOTSTILE PARK.	
	Train de-ray Station at WETHERSFIELD.	
" 5th	Wagon RENDEZVOUS at ABBOTSTILE ?	
" 6th	Pioneer TIMBELL Passed in Command to the 107th Provisional Battalion.	J. Mrs.
	Church Parade.	J. Mrs.
	Starting Medical Board 2 P.M.	K. ors
	Visit from Settle Inspector Dental Officer 3 army	J.P.M.
		N.ors
" 7	Lecture by Capt. Matthews (and Poultry Roads Australia).	K. M.
	Inspector by A.D. M.S. 3 Army by Col. Lee.	
" 8.	Medical Board. (4 standing, 1 sitting, 1 travelling.)	J. Mrs.

WAR DIARY
or
INTELLIGENCE SUMMARY.
(Erase heading not required.)

Army Form C. 2118.

Hour, Date, Place	Summary of Events and Information	Remarks and references to Appendices
Order of BRAINTREE	Field training. Roll overend.	
	B Rn tor Miss Chapman attached.	
10	3 horses 16.0.34. 16.0.35, 1 ammunition transport	MOS
	& 2 k- lorries of Mules.	
11	Secret Instructions (verbal) received for D.A.D.S.	MOS
	to Mobile Brigade	
	Church Parade.	
12	Medical Board. 2 P.M.	MOS
13	Medical Board 2.P.M.	MOS
15	Horse sold by order of A.D.V.S. in BRAINTREE MARKET. MOS	

Army Form C. 2118.

WAR DIARY
or
INTELLIGENCE SUMMARY.
(Erase heading not required.)

Instructions regarding War Diaries and Intelligence Summaries are contained in F.S. Regs., Part II. and the Staff Manual respectively. Title pages will be prepared in manuscript.

Hour, Date, Place	Summary of Events and Information	Remarks and references to Appendices
No.2. 18th BRAMAFE	Fourfret Winkerley G. Duthie & 60th Divn arrived from Newington.	K.D.S.
19 " "	S.O.T. covers chicel paigh	K.D.S
20 " "	Nicholas Road	K.D.S.
21 " "	Alarm exercise. 1st Airport. Alarm 7.02. 6.20 am 2nd aircraft raft huge off Mitcalvin 9.30 a.m. Fourfret Equinoctial attacked from L.P.o. hrs late. Detail Torpedo across 7½ hrs late.	K.M.S
22. "	Relay called in & stared all ranks pt. keyt Scene. Review & tograms	K.M.K
23. " "	Inspector of G.O.C. 60th Divn (Genl Boem) 2nd in command without seen turn. Funeral. 7 enemy.	K.D.S
" "	Glorious November. 500 turn on Nairfort four - water tag food	K.D.S

(73989) W4141—463. 400,000. 9/14. H.&J.Ltd. Forms/C. 2118/10.

WAR DIARY or INTELLIGENCE SUMMARY.

Army Form C. 2118.

Hour, Date, Place	Summary of Events and Information	Remarks and references to Appendices
December 24 1915. BRENTREE	Sgt WATSON. W.R. A.S.C. att. detailed for survey of GHQ body. Passed kit inspection. Refund receipt card of Lifthlleen (civilian) at WITHAM. Bol Sunday Offr W.Officer instructed unit to 2/14 Batts. being detailed from Wincester claim over leave out.	
	Capt. MINETT, Lieut WETHERED proceeded on 4 days sheep-skin care.	KMS
25	being wet. Men from 2 pln. (Ref) P.S. Men most of whom he looked after also on detach 24).	
	H.M. the King through all and during dinner at the Hospital near there	K.M.S

Army Form C. 2118.

WAR DIARY
or
INTELLIGENCE SUMMARY.
(Erase heading not required.)

Instructions regarding War Diaries and Intelligence
Summaries are contained in F.S. Regs., Part II.
and the Staff Manual respectively. Title pages
will be prepared in manuscript.

Hour, Date, Place	Summary of Events and Information	Remarks and references to Appendices
August 26 - BRAINTREE	Pte WALEFORD, WATTS, RAINBOW & Cpl MARTIN Church Parade.	
27 "	Holiday granted by O.C. 161. Brigade	
28	Lt Col MORLEY returns from course of lectures. Instruction — (it occurs there has been a rear excessive number missing). 1/6hr	
	Inoculated 143 NCO Men at (COGGESHALL 77 Men. Relief been fit & Hope Lucas alter 9.7 Age 100°. 30 Army Postal Bag / Zen Hue A(9/—) (windows of telegraph) 1 kw and Light Bracelets Capt CURRAN, 2/ Middle BOARD. opened. 3 missing at 3 rowing	furt
P.M.	The same return asked for & full head phases. Page 1 (envelope by telegraph)	nm

WAR DIARY
or
INTELLIGENCE SUMMARY.
(Erase heading not required.)

Army Form C. 2118.

Hour, Date, Place	Summary of Events and Information	Remarks and references to Appendices
1915		
Dec. 20. Tarentaise.	Pieces & accers concentrated at Bo Field Park. Marched into Bryne Kill of 2.11 4.23. 1.4 Do G.H. S.F.E J.Army attached also [?] & 80 & Divs later entered concentrating in open park close to Rouge J aeroplanes — also pieces Pack Guard were inadequate. Toulouse (none) Shelter was sub sell for 10 lorries till 2.11 Dec 21. EGGERTA LL. White lines More Nov 4-30.	a theuri [?] MSR.

Army Form C. 2118.

WAR DIARY
or
INTELLIGENCE SUMMARY.
(Erase heading not required.)

Instructions regarding War Diaries and Intelligence Summaries are contained in F.S. Regs., Part II. and the Staff Manual respectively. Title pages will be prepared in manuscript.

Hour, Date, Place	Summary of Events and Information	Remarks and references to Appendices
1/5/15	Inspection of Beating Clothing & been etc. Capt W. SCARISBRICK, M.D. for Romand Field Ambulance reports unfit of duty. C.O. this visit Gonio Case for Ileatiny. & urgent private business. Capt MATTHEWS in command with Capt MINTON acting adjutant. Pte MAKINS sent this morning to TAM's & Pte [illegible] Should outside work — 3 cases admitted A.O.E. Rev Batt arrived after 8 MATINS 6/Cerks	[signature] Major R.A.M.C. Commanding 2/4th London Field Ambulance.

(2)

2/6th. London Field Ambulance.

Operation Orders for December 30th. 1915

Major. J.E.B.Wells.

Reference O.S.½" No.30

Any Map of Eastern Counties.	1 (a)	A Grey Invading Force has landed on NORFOLK Coast and is moving on LONDON.
	(b)	The 60th London Division is ordered to concentrate at HAVERHILL
	2	The 181st Infantry Brigade (less the 2/22nd Battalion London Regiment) will concentrate at GOSFIELD PARK to-morrow en route to HAVERILL. Rendezvous Eastern Entrance of the Park.
	3	The troops in Braintree will march at 10 a.m. at which hour the head of the Main Body will pass the Starting Point.
	4	The Starting Point will be the MILL in BOCKING
181st Brigade Machine Guns 2/23rd London Reg, (less one Company) 2/23th London Reg, (less one Company) 2/24th.London Reg. (less one company) Echelon B first line Transport under Command of Senior Transport Officer 2/6th. London Field Ambulance. Divisional Train in order of march of Units 181st.Brig.A.S.C. The O.S. Commanding A.S.C. Commanding the last two	5	The 2/6th London Field Ambulance will accompany the Main Body. Order of March as in the margin.
	6	Further orders will be issued at the rendezvous

Issued at 7 a.m.
Copy No.1 Filed
Copy No.2 A.D.M.S.
Copy No.3 Brig.Head.Qtrs.
Copy No.4 War Diary

Major Ramey
.... Commanding.
Field Ambulance.

Appendix A.

181st INFANTRY BRIGADE

---o---

BRIGADE EXERCISE DECEMBER 2nd

1. The Brigade will concentrate for drill on Thursday, 2nd December at ABBOTS HALL (1 mile South of SHALFORD) at 12.15 p.m.

2. POSITION OF ASSEMBLY - immediately South of the second gate of the North entrance to the Park; Adjutants and brigade markers to report at that spot at 12 noon.

3. FORMATION - line of battalions in Mass facing South in the order from right to left :-
       2/22nd   2/24th   2/23rd   2/21st
   The 2/6th Field Amb. R.A.M.C. and No.4 Company A.S.C. will be on the left of the Brigade in the order named

4. Battalions and the 2/6th London Field Ambulance R.A.M.C., and No.4 Company A.S.C. will march by the following routes :-

2/21st Bn. London Regt	COGGESHALL - TUMBLER'S GREEN - BOCKING CHURCH STREET - GREAT CODHAM HALL - East Gate ABBOTS HALL.
2/22nd Bn. London Regt	DUNMOW - BLAKE END - GREAT SALING - SHALFORD GREEN - CHURCH END - North Gate ABBOTS HALL.
2/23rd Bn. London Regt	BRAINTREE - East Gate ABBOTS HALL (returning via SHALFORD GREEN and RAYNE)
2/24th Bn. London Regt	BRAINTREE - RAYNE - SHALFORD GREEN - CHURCH END - North Gate ABBOTS HALL (returning direct to BRAINTREE)
No.6 Field Ambulance R.A.M.C.	BRAINTREE - East Gate ABBOTS HALL and return.
No.4 Company A.S.C.	Will follow the route taken by the 2/24th Battalion both on the out and return journeys

5. Transport to be fully loaded each wagon etc. to have a card affixed showing contents.

BRAINTREE
29-11-15

Captain
Brigade Major
181st Infantry Brigade

Appendix (B.)

O.P.N. 6

181st Brigade Order No. 2.

Ref. ½" Map
Sheet 30.

CLOCK TOWER
BRAINTREE
20. 12. 15.

1. The Brigade (less 2/22nd Battalion London Regiment) will concentrate at STISTED PARK at 11.30 a.m.

2. The Starting Point will be Road Junction immediately WEST of the "B" in BRAINTREE.

Advanced Guard
Commander
  Major H.Dewsbury
Troops
  2 Companies
  2/24th Bn.L.R.

3. The Advanced Guard (Troops as per margin) will be clear of the Starting Point by 9.50 a.m.

Main Body.
Brigade Hdqrs.
Sect:60th Divl.
Sig:Co:R.E.
2/24th Bn.L.R.
  (less 2 Coys)
Brigade Machine Guns
2/23rd Bn. L.R.
  (less 1 Platoon)
2/6th Lon: Field Amb.
Brigade Train
181st Coy.A.S.C.

4. The Head of the Main Body (Order of March as per margin) will pass the Starting Point at 10 a.m.

5. Route BRAINTREE - JENKINS FARM - HILL - WESTLODGE, STISTED PARK.

Rear Guard.
Commander detailed
  by O.C. 2/23rd
  Bn.Lon.Regt.
1 Platoon 2/23rd
  Bn.Lon.Regt.

6. The 2/21st Battalion London Regiment will concentrate independently.

7. Units Trains (less 2/21st Battalion London Regiment in order of March of Units will be brigaded under the command of Lieut. Dunn, 2/24th Battalion London Regiment.

8. Reports to Head of Main Body -

    After arrival at Position of Assembly to Brigade Headquarters, STISTED PARK.

[signature]
Captain,
Brigade Major,
181st Infantry Brigade.

Issued at 8 P.M.
By
Copy No.1. Filed.
Copy No.2 to 60th Divn. by post 20.12.15.
Copy No.3 to O.C. Sect: 60th Divl Sig:Co: R.E. by Orderly.
Copy No.4 to O.C. Brigade Machine Gun, by Orderly.
Copy No.5 to O.C. Brigade Train, by Orderly.
Copy No.6 to O.C. 2/21st Bn.Lon.Regt. by cycle orderly
Copy No.7 to O.C. 2/23rd Bn.Lon.Regt.)
Copy No.8 to O.C. 2/24th Bn.Lon.Regt.) By Orderly.
Copy No.9 to O.C. 181st Coy A.S.C.)
Copy No.10 to O.C. 2/6th Lon. Field Amb:)

Copy No.10

181st INFANTRY BRIGADE

Order No.1.

SECRET.

PART I.

1. A Concentration of the 181st Brigade (less 2/22nd Battalion London Regiment) will take place on Tuesday 21. 12. 15.

2. Composition of Brigade:-

   Commanding   Colonel C. N. Watts

   Staff Officers   Brigade Staff

   Troops   Sect: 60th Div;Sig:Co:R.E.
                                      181st Infantry Brigade
                                         (less 2/22nd Bn.Lon.Regt
                                      181st Coy: A.S.C.
                                      2/6th London Field Ambce.

3. The Position of Assembly will be STISTED PARK.

4. **Units will commence mobilizing immediately on receipt of order "Concentrate".**

5. Alarm Orders will be acted on so far as they are not modified by Appendix I.

PART II.

Mobilization.	1. (a) All Units will be ready to move from their Unit Alarm Posts at 9.30 a.m.
	(b) Officers Commanding will report when they are so ready.
	By Telephone or Telegraph in the case of the 2/21st Battalion London Regiment.
	All others in writing.
Ammunition.	2. 120 on the Soldier) Calculated on present 100 in Regimental Reserve) state.
Tools.	3. As per Table II page 8 War Establishments T.F. 1915.
Blankets.	4. See Appendix I.
Rations.	5. Units will carry a Haversack Ration.
Transport	6. All available. Cookers will not be taken.

Rear parties	7. No rear parties are to be left with the exception of:-
	    1 Quartermaster)
	    1 Orderly Room Clerk)
	    1 Junior Clerk) Per Battalion.
	    1 Coy Q.M.Sgt. per Coy.)
	    1 Coy Storeman per Company)
	    2 Cooks per Company)
	Other Units in proportion.
	Will remain at Unit Headquarters.

Kit bags.	8. All kit bags will be packed and taken to Company Store Rooms where Orders will be issued regimentally as to their disposal. Second suits of uniform and spare caps, if any, will not be placed in the kit bags but will be stored separately in charge of the Company Quartermaster Sergeants.
Reports.	Reports to Headquarters, 181st Brigade, BRAINTREE till 9.30 a.m., after that to the Head of the Main Body.

APPENDIX I.

Mobilization   6.30 - 7.30 a.m.

1st Hour.

Kits - Spare Clothing   1. Pack kit bags, convey same, spare kits (vide Operation Order No.8 Part II) and one blanket per man to Company Stores.

2nd Blankets.   2. Roll blankets in bundles (10) rope and label - fatigue parties.

Officers Kits.   3. Taken by Servants to Quartermaster's Stores.

Guard and Police.   4. Dismount Guard and Regimental Police.

Mobilization Boxes.   5. Pack Orderly Room Mobilization Boxes.

Rations.   6. Cooks prepare Haversack Rations.

7.30 - 8 a.m.

Breakfast.   Units will have breakfast.

8 a.m. - 9 a.m.

Transport Officer.   1. To send one wagon to Quartermaster's Stores to load Ammunition for distribution to Companies as per indents.

                        2. 2 Wagons (1 per 2 Companies) to load Blankets at Company Stores.

                        3. One Wagon to Quartermaster's Stores to load tools.

                        4. Two Wagons to Quartermaster's Stores to load Regimental Reserve Ammunition.

                        5. One Cart to load Officers Mess and Kits.

                        6. One Medical Cart to Battalion Headquarters for Stretchers, Medical Stores & Orderly Room Boxes.

                        7. Fill two Water Carts.

Fatigue Parties.   Fatigue parties as required to be detailed to load above blankets, ammunition, tools, Officers Mess and kits at Quartermaster's and Company Stores.

Dress.   Pack the Pack, one Blanket inside and Waterproof Sheet outside.

9 am - 9.30 am

Last ½ hour.   1. Fall in, distribute ammunition, issue Haversack Ration, march to Battalion Alarm Posts in order of march.

                        2. Report when ready.

Issued at
By
Copy No.1 Filed.
Copy No.2 60th (London) Division.
Copy No.3 Sect: 60th Divl. Signal Coy.   Copy No.8 O.C. 2/23rd Bn. L.R.
Copy No.4 Brigade Machine Gun Officer.   Copy No.9 O.C. 2/24th Bn. L.R.
Copy No.5 Senior Transport Officer.   Copy No.10 O.C. 181st Bde. Coy.
Copy No.6 O.C. 2/21st Batt. London Regt.   A.S.C.
Copy No.7 O.C. 2/22nd Batt. London Regt.   Copy No.11 O.C. 2/6th Field Amb.

Appendix FAWA

NOTES.

2 Markers per Unit.   1. Adjutants and Markers of all Units (except
          Brigade Train) will meet the Brigade Major
Sect: 60th Divl. at ~~11 a.m.~~ The WEST LODGE, STISTED PARK,
Sig: Co: R.E.   at ~~11 a.m.~~ Markers as per margin.
1 N.C.O. only.   10.30 a.m.

        2. Adjutants will meet their Units at the
        WEST LODGE, STISTED PARK (The Adjutant,
        2/21st Battalion London Regiment will meet
        his Battalion at The EASTERN LODGE, STISTED
        PARK) and conduct them to their respective
        positions.

       3. Units after taking up position will
        Bivouac. Pack animals will be unsaddled.
        Teams outspanned. Latrines to be dug.

The A Corps will not parade

Appendix B.C.
Dec 30th.

Reference O.S. ½" No.
9, and any map of
Eastern Counties.

GENERAL IDEA

KHAKI Home Defence Troops are moving Northwards to the line CAMBRIDGE - IPSWICH to resist the advance on LONDON of a GREY invading force, which has landed on the NORFOLK COAST.

SPECIAL IDEA ----- KHAKI FORCE

The 60th. (London) Division is ordered to concentrate at HAVERHILL on the COLCHESTER - CAMBRIDGE Branch Line of the G.E.Railway.

Copy No. 7

181ST. INFANTRY BRIGADE   Order No. 1.

BRAINTREE
29th. December 1915.

Reference O.S. ½" No. 30
Army map of Eastern
Counties.

1. (a) A Grey Invading Force which has landed on the NORFOLK COAST is moving on LONDON.
   (b) The 60th. (London) Division is ordered to concentrate at HAVERHILL as part of a movement of Home Defence Troops to resist the enemy's advance.
2. The 181st. Infantry Brigade (less the 2/22nd Battalion, London Regiment) will concentrate at GOSFIELD PARK to-morrow en route to HAVERHILL. Rendezvous Eastern Entrance of the Park.
3. The 2/22nd. Battalion, London Regiment will stand fast at DUNMOW with special orders (imaginary)
4. The 2/21st. Battalion, London Regiment will march at 8-45 a.m. ~~the 30th~~ and follow the route COGGESHALL, HOVELS FARM, TUMBLERS GREEN, STISTED RECTORY, BOULTWOODS FARM, ROMAN ROAD.
5. The Troops in BRAINTREE will march at 10 a.m., at which hour the head of the main body will pass the Starting Point.
6. Starting point The MILL in BOOKING.
7. Advanced Guard, composition as in margin.

Advanced Guard
Commander Major Dicks.
2/23rd. Lond. Regt.
Signal Section R.E.
One Company 2/23rd.
Lond. Regt.

Order of March
Brigade Machine Guns
2/23rd. Lond. Regt.
(less one Company)
2/24th. Lond. Regt.
Echelon B. First Line
Transport under command
of Senior Transport
Officer.
No.6 Field Ambulance
Bttn. Trains in order
of march of Units.
181st. Brigade Coy. A.S.C.
The trains and the A.S.C.
under command of O.C.A.S.C.

8. Main body, order of march as in the margin.

9. Reports to head of main body.
10. Further orders will be issued at the rendezvous.

M. Holak
Captain,
Brigade Major,
181st. Infantry Brigade.

Issued at   a.m.
No. 1 Filed.
No. 2 Divl. H.Q.
No. 3 2/21st. Bn. Lond. Regt.
No. 4 2/22nd. Bn. Lond. Regt.
No. 5 2/23rd. Bn. Lond. Regt.
No. 6 2/24th. Bn. Lond. Regt.
No. 7 O.C. 2/6th. Field Ambulance.
No. 8 181st. Coy. A.S.C.
No. 9 O.C. Sig. Coy R.E.

Copy No. 7

181ST. INFANTRY BRIGADE ORDER NO. 2

Reference ½" Manoeuvre
Map Sheet 30.

Rendezvous
EAST GATE
GOSFIELD PARK

30-12-15.

1. The Brigade will halt for dinners till 2 p.m.
2. Battalions and attached Units will form in mass facing West S.W. of EAST GATE in following order from right to left:-

    Brigade Machine Guns.
    2/21st. Battalion
    2/23rd. Battalion
    2/24th. Battalion
    2/6th. London Field Ambulance.
    181st. Brigade Coy. A.S.C.
    2nd. Echelon 1st. Line Transport and Battalion Trains will join their Units and form up in rear of them.

3. Adjutants and Brigade Markers will report to Brigade Major at EAST GATE at 11-40 a.m.

[signature]
Captain,
Brigade Major,
181st. Infantry Brigade.

Issued at

Copies to

No. 1 Filed
2 Divl. H.Q.
3 2/21st. Bn. Lon. Regt.
4 2/22nd. Bn. Lon. Regt.
5 2/23rd. Bn. Lon. Regt.
6 2/24th. Bn. Lon. Regt.
7 O.C. 2/6th. Field Ambulance.
8 181st. Coy A.S.C.
9 O.C. Sig. Coy. R.E.

(4)

2/6th. London Field Ambulance.

Operation Orders for December 30th. 1915

Major. J.N.M.Wells.

Reference O.S.⅙" No.30

Any Map of Eastern Counties.	1 (a)	A Grey Invading Force has landed on NORFOLK Coast and is moving on LONDON.
	(b)	The 60th London Division is ordered to concentrate at HAVERHILL
	2	The 181st Infantry Brigade (less the 2/22nd Battalion London Regiment) will concentrate at GOSFIELD PARK to-morrow en route to HAVERHILL. Rendezvous Eastern Entrance of the Park.
	3	The troops in Braintree will march at 10 a.m. at which hour the head of the Main Body will pass the Starting Point.
	4	The Starting Point will be the MILL in BOCKING

181st Brigade
Machine Guns
2/23rd London Reg.
 (less one Company)
2/23th London Reg.
 (less one Company)
2/24th.London Reg.
 (less one company)
Echelon B first line
 Transport under Command
 of Senior Transport
 Officer
2/6th. London Field
 Ambulance.
Divisional Train in order
of march of Units
181st.Brig.A.S.C.
The O.C. Commanding A.S.C.
 Commanding the last
 two

5 The 2/6th London Field Ambulance will accompany the Main Body. Order of March as in the margin.

6 Further orders will be issued at the rendezvous

Issued at 7 a.m.
Copy No.1 Filed
Copy No.2 A.D.M.S.
Copy No.3 Brig. Head. Qtrs.
Copy No. 4 War Diary.

CONFIDENTIAL

WAR DIARY MARCH 1st to MARCH 31st 1916

2/6th LONDON FIELD AMBULANCE.

Army Form C. 2118.

WAR DIARY
or
INTELLIGENCE SUMMARY.
(Erase heading not required.)

Instructions regarding War Diaries and Intelligence Summaries are contained in F. S. Regs., Part II and the Staff Manual respectively. Title pages will be prepared in manuscript.

Hour, Date, Place	Summary of Events and Information	Remarks and references to Appendices
SUTTON VENY		
1.2.16. 7.am	Physical Drill & Snacks.	
9 am	Route march. BOREHAM - HEYTESBURY WARMINSTER Rd - SACK HILL - BATTLESBURY HILL - PIT 361 - BISHOP TROW HOUSE - HEYTESBURY WARMINSTER Rd - BOREHAM - SUTTON VENY CAMP. Route very bad condition owing to building work.	[sgd]
2.2.16. 7am	Squad Drill & Snacks	
9	Musketry Drill 9-11	
11	Physical Drill 11-12	
2pm	Musketry Drill 2-2.45	
2.45	Drill 2 or 3 m/s from	
3	Lecture in Hut Adj 3-4.	[sgd]

Army Form C. 2118.

WAR DIARY
or
INTELLIGENCE SUMMARY.
(Erase heading not required.)

Instructions regarding War Diaries and Intelligence Summaries are contained in F.S. Regs., Part II. and the Staff Manual respectively. Title pages will be prepared in manuscript.

Hour, Date, Place	Summary of Events and Information	Remarks and references to Appendices
ATTUNVENY		
3-2-11 7pm	Orgnd Drill & clothing.	
9	Orgnd Drill 9-10.	
10	Lectured & Kit inspection 10-12	
	All clothing inspected	
2	Platoon Drill 2-3	
3	Coy Drill 3-4 pm	appn.
4-3-16. 7pm	Genrl Drill & clothing.	
9 am	Platoon Drill 9-11	
11	Orgnd Drill 11-12 noon.	appn

(73989) W4141—463. 400,000. 9/14. H.&J.Ltd. Forms/C. 2118/10.

Army Form C. 2118.

WAR DIARY
or
INTELLIGENCE SUMMARY.
(Erase heading not required.)

Instructions regarding War Diaries and Intelligence Summaries are contained in F.S. Regs., Part II. and the Staff Manual respectively. Title pages will be prepared in manuscript.

Hour, Date, Place	Summary of Events and Information	Remarks and references to Appendices
SUTTON VENY 5.3.16	Church Parade. Roman Catholic 8.45 am Ch. of England 9.5 am Non Conformists 10 am Captain BROWN proceeded to HARROGATE on sick leave 9pm.	
6.3.16 7am 9. 2 PM 3 PM	Snowing & very cold. Dismissed 1st period drill. Musketry drill Physical drill } 9–12 Squad drill Musketry drill 2–3 Drill and Musketry.	attach

(73989) W4141–463. 400,000. 9/14. H.&J.Ltd. Forms/C. 2118/10.

Army Form C. 2118.

WAR DIARY
or
INTELLIGENCE SUMMARY.
(Erase heading not required.)

Instructions regarding War Diaries and Intelligence Summaries are contained in F.S. Regs., Part II. and the Staff Manual respectively. Title pages will be prepared in manuscript.

Hour, Date, Place		Summary of Events and Information	Remarks and references to Appendices
SUTTON VENY 7.3.16	7 am	Donkey & Spud Drill	
	9 am	Stretcher & Sqdn Drill 9–10	
	10 am	Horses, Inoculation	
		Officers Drill	
		Squad Drill & Instr 10–12	
	2 pm	Squad Drill 2–3	
	3 pm	Lecture & Practical Instr on Sqd 3–4	
8.3.16		Lieut METHERED Transferred to T.F. Reserve	
		Capt. WILSON } taken on Strength of Unit	
		Lieut. McDOWELL	
		Lieut. HOWARD	
	7 am	Spud Drill & Cookery	
	9 am	Physical Drill } & Instr 9–11.	
		Squad Drill	

Army Form C. 2118.

WAR DIARY
or
INTELLIGENCE SUMMARY.
(Erase heading not required.)

Hour, Date, Place	Summary of Events and Information	Remarks and references to Appendices
SUTTON VENY 6.3.16 (Mon)	11 Am Lecture on First Aid 11-12	
2 Pm	No Equipment issued to N.C.O.s & men forming [struck through]	JPPR
7.3.16. 7 Am	Squad Drill & smoking	
9 Am	Field Training 9-12.30	
2.30	Physical Drill 2.30-3	
3 Pm	Lecture on First Aid	
	Captain WILSON and Lieut HOWARD left for LONDON to attend Course of Lectures on the 10th & 11th inst at MILLBANK.	JPPR

WAR DIARY
or
INTELLIGENCE SUMMARY.
(Erase heading not required.)

Army Form C. 2118.

Hour, Date, Place	Summary of Events and Information	Remarks and references to Appendices
SUTTON VENY		
10.3.16. 7am	Squad Drill & Dorking	
9am	Physical Drill	
10am	Marched 2 1/2[?] Squads 10-12.	
2pm	Stretch Drill 2-3	
3pm	Gas Antis.	
	Lieut- THORNTON reported for duty & posted to A Sec.	JRM
11.3.16		
7am	Squad Drill & Dorking	
9am	Semaphore Signalling 9-10	
10am	Stretcher & Gym Drill	
	Lieut GLASS appointed Transport Officer	JRM

Army Form C. 2118.

WAR DIARY
or
INTELLIGENCE SUMMARY.
(Erase heading not required.)

Instructions regarding War Diaries and Intelligence Summaries are contained in F.S. Regs., Part II. and the Staff Manual respectively. Title pages will be prepared in manuscript.

Hour, Date, Place	Summary of Events and Information	Remarks and references to Appendices
SUTTON VENY 12.3.16	Church Parades:- Roman Catholics 7.45 am Church of England 9.5 am Non Conformists 10 am L/Sgt. CUNNINGHAM returned for limitation trade	MM
13.3.16	7 am Squad Drill & Orderly 9 am Field Training 9 - 12.30 Wet & very cold. 2 pm Platoon Drill 2 - 3 3 Lecture on Fast Aid 2nd. HOWARD transferred to 2/5 devon Field Amb, to take off the charge of this unit.	MM

(73989) W4141—463. 400,000. 9/14. H.&J.Ltd. Forms/C. 2118/10.

WAR DIARY
or
INTELLIGENCE SUMMARY.

(Erase heading not required.)

Army Form C. 2118.

Hour, Date, Place	Summary of Events and Information	Remarks and references to Appendices
SUTTON VENY 14.3.16	7am Physical Drill	
	9am Lecture 9-10	
	10am Musketry + Extr Drill	
	2pm Company Drill 2-3	
	3pm Bn [?] and Parade 5pm	
15.3.16	7am Squad Drill & Bombing	
	9am Route march	
	Major CORFE, Capt MATHEWS, Sgt Majr PEARSON & Sgts PULVERMACHER, JONES, P & KING attached Inf to Gas Lecture + Demonstration	
	2pm Clothing Inspection by Lieut GLASS	
	3pm Bn Anti Gas Lecture	

Army Form C. 2118.

WAR DIARY
or
INTELLIGENCE SUMMARY.
(Erase heading not required.)

Instructions regarding War Diaries and Intelligence Summaries are contained in F.S. Regs., Part II. and the Staff Manual respectively. Title pages will be prepared in manuscript.

Hour, Date, Place	Summary of Events and Information	Remarks and references to Appendices
SUTTON VENY		
16. 3. 16.	Programme of Training continued	Appendix A
17. 3. 16	do	App
18. 3. 16	do	App
19. 3. 16	Church Parade 9.5. am.	App
20. 3. 16	Training as L weekly programme.	Appendix B.
21. 3. 16	Field & winn postponed owing to heavy rain	App
	Physical Drill & Drill and Substituted	
22. 3. 16	Route march postponed owing to weather	
	Physical Drill & Musketry Typically - 9-12	
2 PM	Route march.	

WAR DIARY
or
INTELLIGENCE SUMMARY.
(Erase heading not required.)

Army Form C. 2118.

Hour, Date, Place		Summary of Events and Information	Remarks and references to Appendices
SUTTON VENY			
23.3.16	6pm	Training as in programme	
		B Section under Captn MATTHEWS took part in 1st Brigade Field Training	
24.3.16	6pm	Training as in programme. Orders received from A.D.M.S. for Officer & squad of men to attend at Range daily	
25.3.16	6pm	Training as in programme.	
26.3.16		Church Parade 6.20 AM	
27.3.16	6pm	Training as in programme	Appendix C.
28.3.16	6pm	Training severely interfered with by weather conditions. Snow, rain & high wind.	

WAR DIARY
or
INTELLIGENCE SUMMARY.
(Erase heading not required.)

Army Form C. 2118.

Hour, Date, Place	Summary of Events and Information	Remarks and references to Appendices
SUTTON VENY		
29.3.16	Weekly programme of training	attach
30.3.16	" " "	attach
31.3.16	" " "	attach

PROGRAMME OF TRAINING 2/4th. LONDON FIELD AMBULANCE.   Week ending 1st.April 1916

Day	7.0–7.45 a.m.	9.0–12.30 p.m.	2.0–3.0 p.m.	3.0–4.0 p.m.	Remarks
Monday	Squad drill and 30 min.run	Field Training with M.G. of Minimum Deployment	Stretcher Drill (Whistle and Signal)	First Aid	Staff Employed Physical drill 5.0–5.30 p.m. daily except Saturdays
Tuesday	Physical drill	Demonstration or Lecture (9.0–10.0 a.m.) Stretcher Drill & Wagon Drill (10.0–12.0)	Company Drill	First Aid	Recruits classes First Aid 4.0–5.0 daily and Saturday Morning
Wednesday	Squad drill and Musketry	Route March (with stretchers) (Route to leave at Wagon Lines at 9.15 a.m.)	Stretcher Drill with refused limbs and improvised Litters	First Aid	
Thursday	Physical drill	Tent pitching (Sworkston Hill)	Company Drill	First Aid	
Friday	Squad drill and Running	Field ambulance drill (9.15–12.0) March and its Inspection	Equipment of Field Ambulance Vehicles	First Aid	Full Field Dress
Saturday	Medical drill	Demonstration or Lecture (Visual Fire control Voice eat-driel & Signal Passage Trumpet (10.–11.0) Semaphore Signalling (11.0–12.0)			Place No 2 Camp Uniform unless otherwise stated

PROGRAMME OF TRAINING :- 2/6th London Field Ambulance. Week-ending 25th March 1916M

DAY.	7-0 to 7-45	9-0 to 12-30	2-0 to 3-0	3-0 to 4-0	Remarks.
MONDAY.	Squad Drill Doubling 300 yards.	Field Training.	Stretcher Drill (Whistle & Signal)	First Aid.	Staff Employed. Physical Drill.
TUESDAY.	Physical Drill	Demonstration or Lecture (9-0 to 10-0), Stretcher Drill, & Wagon Drill 10-0 to 12-0)	Company Drill.	First Aid	2-0 to 2-30 daily except Saturday. === ===
WEDNESDAY	Squad Drill and Doubling.	Route March (with Transport) (Road N,N.E. from Heytesbury past East Hill Farm.)	Stretcher Drill (With reduced numbers)	First Aid	Backward classes First Aid
Thursday.	Physical Drill	Field Training (On Cotley Hill N.W. of Heytesbury.)	Company Drill.	First Aid.	4-0 to 4-30 daily except saturday. =======
FRIDAY.	Squad Drill & Doubling	Field Ambulance Drill (9-0 to 10-0) Health & Kit Inspection (10-0 to 12-0)	Equipment Loading Technical vehicles.	Pay.	Baths allotted Fridays. ==========
SATURDAY.	Physical Drill	DEMONSTRATION or Lecture (9-0 to 10-0) Hand seat drill and improvised carriage of wounded(10-11).			Place:- No.2 Camp unless otherwise stated. ==========

PROGRAMME OF TRAINING FOR WEEK ENDING 18th MARCH 1916.

2/6th London Field Ambulance. 60th London Division.

DAY.	7-0 to 7-45	9-0 to 12-30	2-0 -3-0	3-0 to 4-0
MONDAY.	Squad Drill and Doubling, (300 yds)	Field Training.	Stretcher Drill (by whistle & signal)	First Aid.
TUESDAY.	Physical Drill.	Demonstration or Lecture (9-0 to 10-0) Stretcher and Wagon Drill (10-0 to 12-0)	Company Drill.	First Aid.
WEDNESDAY.	Squad Drill & Doubling	Route March (with Transport)	Stretcher Drill (with reduced numbers)	First Aid.
THURSDAY.	Physical Drill.	Field Training.	Company Drill.	First Aid.
FRIDAY.	Squad Drill and Doubling.	Field Ambulance Drill (9-0 to 10-0) Health & Kit Inspection (10-0 to 12-0)	Equipment Loading Technical vehicles.	Pay. (Baths allotted.)
SATURDAY.	Physical Drill.	Demonstration or Lecture (9-0 to 10-0) Hand seat Drill & improvised carriage of Wounded. Semaphore Signalling 11-12.		

CONFIDENTIAL.

WAR DIARY APRIL 1st to APRIL 30th 1916

2/6th LONDON FIELD AMBULANCE

2/6th LONDON FIELD AMBULANCE. WEEK-ENDING 29th APRIL 1916.

PROGRAMME OF TRAINING

Day.	7-0 a.m. to 7-45 a.m.	9-0 a.m. to 12-30 p.m.	2-0 p.m. to 3-0 p.m.	3-0 p.m. to 4-0 P.M.	Remarks.
Monday.	——	Route March until 4-0 p.m. via, Sutton Veny, Cockerton Green and Longleat Park.			
Tuesday.	Physical Drill.	Lecture (9-0 to 10-0) Stretcher Drill & Wagon Drill 10-0 to 12-0)	Lecture by C.O. from 2-0 to 4-0		
Wednesday.	Physical Drill.	Field Training (9-0 a.m. to 4-0 p.m. Tytherington Hill.			
Thursday.	Squad Drill & Doubling	Tent pitching 9-0 a.m. Stretcher Drill by whistle and signal (10-0 12-0)	Company Drill	First Aid	
Friday	Physical Drill.	Field Training.	Kit and Medical Inspection.	Pay.	
Saturday.	——	~~Route March 8-0 to 11-0 p.m.~~ More of No. 9 Camp.			

.... Major, R.A.M.C.(T)
O.C. 2/6th London Field Ambulance.

Sutton Veny

Appendix "D"

PROGRAMME OF TRAINING 2/6th London Field Ambulance Week-ending April 22nd 1916.

Day.	7-20 a.m. to 7-50 a.m.	9-0 a.m. to 12-30 p.m.	2-0 p.m. to 3-0	3-0 p.m. to 4-0 p.m.	Remarks.
Monday.		Tactical Exercise			Staff Employed Physical Drill 3-0 to 3-30 every day except Saturday.
Tuesday.	Physical Drill	Demonstration 9-10 Stretcher & Wagon Drill 10-12	Company Drill		
Wednesday.	Squad Drill & Doubling.	Route March (with Transport)	Equipment & Panniers	First Aid	
Thursday.	Physical Drill.	Field Training	Company Drill.	First Aid	
Friday.		Church Parade & Pay Duties.			Baths allotted Fridays.
Saturday.	Physical Drill	Demonstration or Lecture (9-0 to 10-0 a.m.) Hand seat drill and Improvised Carriage of Wounded with Application. (11-0 to 12-0)			

R Corpe Major
o/c. 2/6th London Field Ambulance.

2nd/6th LONDON
16 APR 1916
FIELD AMBULANCE (T.)

PROGRAMME OF TRAINING. 2/6th London Field Ambulance. Week-ending April 15th, 1916.

Day	7.0 a.m. to 7.45 a.m.	9.0 a.m. to 12.30 p.m.	2.0 p.m. to 3.0 p.m.	3.0 p.m. to 4.0 p.m.	REMARKS
MONDAY	Squad Drill and Doubling 300 yds	Field Training on area between Scratchbury Hill and Cotley Hill	Stretcher Drill (Whistle & Signal)	First Aid	Staff Employed Physical Drill 2.0 to 2.30 every day except Saturday
TUESDAY	Physical Drill	Demonstration or Lecture (9.0 to 10.0 a.m.) Stretcher Drill and Wagon Drill (10.0 to 12.0)	Company Drill	First Aid	Backward classes First Aid (4.0 to 4.30 p.m. except Saturday)
WEDNESDAY		DIVISIONAL EXERCISES FOR MEDICAL UNITS			
THURSDAY	Physical Drill	Lecture on first Aid 9.0-10.0 Stretcher and Wagon Drill (10.0 to 12.0)	Company Drill	First Aid	
FRIDAY	Squad Drill and Doubling	Route March-Tythington-Point 327-Salisbury Warminster Road Hytesbury	Health and Kit Inspection	Pay Duties	Baths allotted Fridays
SATURDAY	Physical Drill	Demonstration or Lecture (9.0 to 10.0 a.m.) Hand seat Drill and Improvised Carriage of Wounded (10.0-12.0) Semaphore signalling (11.0-12.0)			Place No. 2 Camp, unless otherwise stated

PROGRAMME OF TRAINING 2/6th London Field Ambulance.   Week-ending April 8th 1916.

Day.	7.0 to 7.45 a.m.	9.0 to 11.45.	2.0 to 3.45 p.m.	3.0 to 4.0 p.m.	Remarks.
Sunday.	Squad drill and marching.	Field training. Stretcher drill.	Stretcher drill. Mobile Section (instruction). Dispatch loading (instruction).	First Aid.	Staff employed. Physical Drill 7.0 to 8.0 every day except Saturday.
Monday.	Physical drill.	Demonstration of Lecture (9.0 to 1045 a.m.) Stretcher drill & wagon drill. (11.0 to 11.45 a.m.)	Company drill.	First Aid.	Squad classes First Aid 6.40 to 7.30 p.m. except Saturday.
Tuesday.	Squad drill and marching.	Route March (with Transport) Stretcher and Company later. Slade Park-Longworth-Denerhill.	Stretcher drill (Instruction) Dispatch loading (Demonstr.)	First Aid.	
Wednesday.	Physical drill.	Field training. Lord's Hill-Hill Top of Road.	Company drill.	First aid.	
Thursday.	Squad drill and marching.	Field Ambulance drill. (9.0 to 10.45 a.m.) Route & Kit inspection.	Stretcher drill. (Route Section.) Dispatch loading (Demonstr.)	No lecture.	Leave allowed Fridays.
Friday.	Physical drill.	Recreation or Lecture (9.0 to 10.45 a.m.) Squad and drill and if impractical Carriage of wounded (500 entries) Semaphore signalling (11.0 to 12.0)			Leave. Inspection. Officers classes.

O/C 2/6th London Field Ambulance.

Major Ra m c (T)

Appendix "A"

Army Form C. 2118.

WAR DIARY
or
INTELLIGENCE SUMMARY.
(Erase heading not required.)

Instructions regarding War Diaries and Intelligence Summaries are contained in F.S. Regs., Part II. and the Staff Manual respectively. Title pages will be prepared in manuscript.

Hour, Date, Place	Summary of Events and Information	Remarks and references to Appendices
SUTTON VENY		
1.4.16 9pm	Drew Extra 9-10 Special Parade of wounded 10-11 Lymphine & gassing 11-12	
2.4.16 am	Church Parade	
3.4.16 to 8.4.16	Training as in programme	Appendix 'A'
9.4.16 to 15.4.16	Training as in programme	Appendix 'B'
16.4.16 to 22.4.16	Training as in programme	Appendix 'C'
17.4.16	Major J.W. BIRD. D.S.O. took over command of Bn.	

(73989) W4141—463. 400,000. 9/14. H.&J.Ltd. Forms/C. 2118/10.

Army Form C. 2118.

WAR DIARY
or
INTELLIGENCE SUMMARY.
(Erase heading not required.)

Hour, Date, Place	Summary of Events and Information	Remarks and references to Appendices
SUTTON VENY		
22.4.16 to 28.4.16	Training as in programme	Appendix "D." seen
29.4.16	Unit moved from its position in No.2 Camp to No.9 Camp, allotted to (?) to the medical units of the 60th London Division.	seen
30.4.16	Church Parade	seen

Army Form C. 2118.

WAR DIARY
or
INTELLIGENCE SUMMARY.
(Erase heading not required.)

Instructions regarding War Diaries and Intelligence Summaries are contained in F.S. Regs., Part II. and the Staff Manual respectively. Title pages will be prepared in manuscript.

Hour, Date, Place	Summary of Events and Information	Remarks and references to Appendices

(73989) W4141—463. 400,000. 9/14. H.&J.Ltd. Forms/C. 2118/10.

CONFIDENTIAL.

War Diary. May 1st to May 31. 1916.
2/6th London Field Ambulance.

Programme of Training.   2/6th London Field Training. Week END MAY 6th 1916

Day.	7-0 to 7-45 a.m.	9-0 to 12-0	2-0 to 3-0 p.m.	3-0 to 4-0 p.m.	Remarks
Monday	Physical Drill.	Field training Littlecombe Hill. (9-0 to 4-0)			
Tuesday.	Squad Drill & Doubling.	Stretcher & Wagon Drill (9-0 to 10-30) Morse signalling (10-30 to 12-0)	First Aid Catechism	Stretcher Drill (Whistle & signal)	
Wednesday.	Physical Drill.	Brigade Route March.			
Thursday.	Squad Drill & Doubling.	Field Training Lords Hill.	Lecture	First Aid.	
Friday.	Physical Drill.	Route March	Lecture	Pay Duties.	
Saturday.	Squad Drill & Doubling	Lecture (9-0 to 10-0) First Aid (10-0 to 12-0)	DIVISIONAL SPORTS.		

Sutton Veny
29/4/16

N.R.Watkins
.................Capt. R.A.M.C. (T).
For; C.O. 2/6th London Field Ambulance.

PROGRAMME of TRAINING for Week ending 13th May, 1916.   2/6th LONDON FIELD AMBULANCE.

Day	7.0 a.m. - 7.30	9.0 a.m. - 12.0 noon	2.0 - 3.0	3.0 - 4.0	Remarks.
MONDAY		Route March 9.0 a.m. till 4.0 p.m. via Longbridge Deverill, Warminster, Upton Scudamore, Brick Hill.			
TUESDAY	Physical Drill	Loading of Technical Vehicles	Stretcher Drill	First Aid	
WEDNESDAY	Squad Drill and Doubling	Field Training Tytherington Hill		Lecture	
THURSDAY		Route March 9.0 a.m. till 1.0 p.m. Via Sutton Veny, Corton, Upton Lovell, Heytesbury			
FRIDAY	Physical Drill	9.0 - 11.0 Loading Technical Vehicles 11.0 - 12.0 Morse Signalling	Medical Inspection	Examination First Aid	
SATURDAY	INTERNAL ECONOMY			Pay	

2/6th London Field Ambulance.

W.Bird.

PROGRAMME OF TRAINING. for WEEK ending 20th MAY. 2/6th London Field Ambce

	7.0.t 9..45	9.0.t 12.0	20.t 5 Ⓟ	3 t 4.	Remarks
May 1st 15	Lectur Parade.	← Route March. →			
" 16	"	Stretcher Drill Loading Technical Vehicle	Lecture	Pro Inval Aid	
" 17	Physical Drill	S.'C° Drill	"	"	
" 18	Squad Drill	Field Training Tythenington Hall	—	Lecture	
" 19.	Physical Drill	Co. Drill Smoke Helmet Drill Morse Signalling	Med Inspection	Day.	
" 20.	Lectur Parade	Medical Economy	—	—	

PROGRAMME OF TRAINING.   WEEK ENDING MAY 27th 1916.

DAY.	7-0 a.m. to 7-45 a.m.	9-0 a.m. to 12-30 p.m.	2-0 p.m. to 3-0 p.m.	3-0 p.m. to 4-0 p.m.
Monday 22/5/16	Physical Drill	Stretcher Drill 9-0 to 10-30 Loading Vehicles 10-30 to 12-0	Lecture	Practical 1st Aid
Tuesday 23/5/16		R O U T E M A R C H (9-0 to 12-0 noon)	Lecture	First Aid
Wednesday 24/5/16		D I V I S I O N A L T R A I N I N G.		
Thursday 25/5/16	Squad & Doubling	Company Drill 9-0 to 10-0 Smoke Helmet Drill 10-11-0 Morse Signalling 11-0 to 12-0 noon.	Kit and Medical Inspection.	Pay Duties.
Friday 26/5/16		D I V I S I O N A L T R A I N I N G.		
Saturday 27/5/16		I N T E R N A L E C O N O M Y.		

Sutton Veny
20/5/16.

[signature]
............For Major, R.A.M.C.(T).
Capt, O.C. 2/6th London Field Ambulance.

Programme of Training for end of May 30th. 2/6 Hodson Amber

	7.0 to 7.45	9.0. 6.v.a.	2. 6 – 3	3 to 4	Remarks
May 29	Lechin Parade	Route March → ~			
" 30	Divisional Rehearsal for His Majesty the Kings Inspection.				

Army Form C. 2118.

WAR DIARY
or
INTELLIGENCE SUMMARY.
(Erase heading not required.)

Instructions regarding War Diaries and Intelligence Summaries are contained in F.S. Regs., Part II. and the Staff Manual respectively. Title pages will be prepared in manuscript.

Hour, Date, Place	Summary of Events and Information	Remarks and references to Appendices

(73989) W4141—463. 400,000. 9/14. H.&J.Ltd. Forms/C. 2118/10.

Army Form C. 2118.

WAR DIARY
or
INTELLIGENCE SUMMARY.
(Erase heading not required.)

Instructions regarding War Diaries and Intelligence Summaries are contained in F.S. Regs., Part II. and the Staff Manual respectively. Title pages will be prepared in manuscript.

Hour, Date, Place	Summary of Events and Information	Remarks and references to Appendices
SUTTON VENY		
1.5.16 to 6.5.16	Training as in programme	Appendix "A" attached
7.5.16 to 13.5.16.	Training as in programme	Appendix "B" attached
14.5.16 to 6. 20.5.16	Training as in programme	Appendix "C" attached
21.5.16 to 27.5.16	Training as in programme	Appendix "D" attached

(73989) W4141—463. 400,000. 9/14. H.&J.Ltd. Forms/C. 2118/10.

WAR DIARY
or
INTELLIGENCE SUMMARY.
(Erase heading not required.)

Army Form C. 2118.

Hour, Date, Place	Summary of Events and Information	Remarks and references to Appendices
SUTTON VENY 23. 5- 16.	Capt CLEGG reported for duty and posted to "C" Section.	Appx
29. 5. 16 and 30. 5. 16	Training as in programme	Appendix "E" Prog.
31. 5. 16.	Inspection of 60th London Division by His Majesty THE KING	Appx

CONFIDENTIAL.

WAR DIARY JUNE 1st to JUNE 22nd 1916.

2/6th LONDON FIELD AMBULANCE.

2/6th LONDON FIELD AMBULANCE. PROGRAMME OF TRAINING FOR WEEK ENDING JUNE 3rd 1916.

DAY.	7-0 a.m. to 7-45 a.m.	9-0 a.m. to 12-30 p.m.	2-0 p.m. to 3-0 p.m.	3-0 p.m. to 4-0 p.m.
MONDAY 29/5/16	(Section Parade)	ROUTE MARCH 9-0 to 4-0		
TUESDAY 30/5/16	Physical Drill	Loading Technical Vehicles.	Lecture	First Aid.
WEDNESDAY 31/5/16	Physical Drill	Stretcher Drill 9-0 a.m. to 10-30 a.m. Lecture 10-30 a.m. to 12 noon	First Aid	Signalling
THURSDAY 1/6/1916	Physical Drill	Morse Signalling 9-0 to 10-0 Gas Helmet Drill 10-0 to 11-0 Lecture 11-0 to 12-0 noon	Examination first aid.	
FRIDAY 2/6/1916.	------	ROUTE MARCH 9-0 to 3-0		Pay.
SATURDAY 3/6/1916.	Physical Drill	INTERNAL ECONOMY.		

Appendix "A"

Programme of Training.   2/6th London Field Ambulance.   Week Ending 16th. 1916

Day	7-0 a.m. to 7-30 a.m.	9-0 a.m. to 12-30 p.m.	2-0 p.m. to 3-0 p.m.	3-0 p.m. to 4-0 p.m.
Monday	Physical Drill	Stretcher Drill 9-0 to 10-0 Gas Helmet Drill 10-0 to 11-0 Morse Signalling 11-0 to 12-0	Lecture	First Aid.
Tuesday	Physical Drill	Inspection of Kit Issue of Clothing etc.	Stretcher Drill	First Aid.
Wednesday	Physical Drill	Loading Ambulance Wagons 9-0 to 11-0 Stretcher Drill 11-0 to 12-0	First Aid	Signalling
Thursday	---	Route March 9-0 a.m. to 4-0 p.m.		
Friday	Physical Drill	Morse Signalling 9-0 to 10-0 Gas Helmet Drill 10-0 to 11-0 Loading Ambulance Wagons 11-0 to 12-0	Lecture	Pay.
Saturday	Physical Drill	Internal Economy		

Sutton Very
10/6/1916.

..................Major, R.A.M.C.(T).
O.C. 2/6th London Field Ambulance.

Appendix "A"

PROGRAMME OF TRAINING   2/6th. London Field Ambulance.   Week Ending 9th. June. 1916

Day	7.0 a.m. to 7.30 a.m.	9.0 a.m. to 12.30 p.m.	2.0 p.m. to 3.0 p.m.	3.0 p.m. to 4.0 p.m.
Monday	Physical Drill	Stretcher Drill 9.0-10.0 Gas Helmet Drill 10.0-11.0 Morse Signalling 11.0-12.0	Lecture	First Aid
Tuesday	*Physical Drill*	~~Route March~~ *Inspection of Kit — 9.0 a.m. to Issue of new Clothing - etc.*	*Lecture — 4.0 p.m. Stretcher Drill*	*First Aid*
Wednesday	Physical Drill	Loading Ambulance Wagons 9.0 - 11.0 Stretcher Drill 11.0- 12.0	First Aid	Signalling
Thursday	————	Route March 9.0 a.m. to 4.0 p.m.		
Friday	Physical Drill	Morse Signalling 9.0-10.0 Gas Helmet Drill 10.0-11.0 Loading Ambulance Wagons 11.0-12.0	Lecture	Pay
Saturday	Physical Drill	Internal Economy		

M. Buck.
O.C. 2/6 London Field Ambulance.

Major RAMC.

Appendix "B"

BH.
2467/16

SUBJECT:- INSTRUCTIONS RE DIVISION
PROCEEDING OVERSEAS.

The following instructions and aids are sent round for the information of all Officers Commanding Units.

This table is made out for period giving notice of departure equal to seven days. The work may have to be done in less and the days can be automatically telescoped.

It will be seen that these arrangements are in two parts showing :-
(1) That the seven days may follow consecutively.
(2) There can be a halt after the 4th day.
(3) They may have to be telescoped - the last three days into the first four.

1st day. Officers Commanding Units to parade all their Officers, men, transport and everything they will take overseas; inspect the same to see that all is in order, and all men present; this is to be done in the forenoon, discrepancies made good in the afternoon and list sent to the D.A.D.O.S.

2nd day. Boards of Survey to be held on clothing.
All clothing to be boarded to be put into two categories.
Condemned clothing to be surveyed by contractor and sold to him.
Clothing still serviceable to be disinfected and returned to depots.
Units will close all their accounts and return all surplus equipment to O.C.Warminster and new clothing to A.O.D. Southampton.
Para.189, Mobilization Regulations - Return Documents to Records.
Para 194 Mobilization Regulations - closing present system of Pay.

3rd day. All personal private property of Officers and men should be collected and removed from the hutments and barracks. This should be done under the personal supervision of Commanding Officers, and Officers Commanding Platoons.

4th day. Return all stores received for instruction and surplus to Mobilization requirements, Peace Stores etc., to Ordnance Warminster, accompanied by vouchers.

Officers Commanding will make the necessary arrangements to have the hutments and fixtures inspected from the point of view of the D.O.R.E. and Officer i/c Barracks.

All stores and tools on loan from the L.O.R.E. including Aylwin Huts, to be returned to R.E. Store, Sutton Veny. Notice of the date and time of return to be sent to D.O.R.E.Wylye Valley, Codford.

Arrangements to be made for patch pockets to be sewn on jackets for overseas.

3rd day before leaving.
All hutments will be thoroughly scrubbed out with Creosole; all rubbish to be burnt and buried.

Supply Officers of the Divisional Train to be responsible that any accumulation of supplies such as groceries,oat sacks, tea tins, packing cases, are returned to the Supply Depot. Officers Commanding Units will afford every facility in this matter by under drawing supplies so as to prevent accumulation.

(- 2 -)

2nd day before leaving.

Inspect Gas Helmets, Feild Dressings, Identity Discs, and Pay Books, etc.

Bed Boards and trestles, and tables and trestles, to be stacked in Dining Rooms, piled ready for easy counting without moving them.

All other Barrack Stores to be stacked in Miniature Rifle Ranges ready for counting.

The Officer Commanding Details to be left behind, will satisfy himself that they are correct.

All blankets, whether on inventory from Officer i/c Barracks or on voucher from Ordnance, should be got ready for return by the O.C. Details to Officer i/c Barracks; those held on charge from Ordnance to be vouchered to Officer i/c Barracks.

The day before leaving:-

A general parade of all ranks in each Unit, as for overseas, fully equipped; during indpection, all private personal effects surplus, left from previous inspection on 3rd day, to be destroyed under supervision of Officers Commanding Unit.

Last day:-

Fuel and Light Account to be accurately closed.

General:-

The first day of Mobilization will be notified in due course.

Reports will be rendered each day by 7 p.m. that the instructions for the day have been carried out.

Appendix "D".

Programme of Training   2/6th London Field Ambulance   Week Ending 16th 1916

Day	7-0 a.m. to 7-30 a.m.	9-0 a.m. to 12-30 p.m.	2-0 p.m. to 3-0 p.m.	3-0 p.m. to 4-0 p.m.
Monday	Physical Drill	Stretcher Drill 9-0 to 10-0 Gas Helmet Drill 10-0 to 11-0 Morse Signalling 11-0 to 12-0	Lecture	First Aid.
Tuesday	Physical Drill	Inspection of Kit Issue of Clothing etc.	Stretcher Drill	First Aid.
Wednesday	Physical Drill	Loading Ambulance Wagons 9-0 to 11-0 Stretcher Drill 11-0 12-0	First Aid	Signalling
Thursday	----	Route March 9-0 a.m. to	4-0 p.m.	
Friday	Physical Drill	Morse Signalling 9-0 to 10-0 Gas Helmet Drill 10-0 to 11-0 Loading Ambulnce Wagons 11-0 to 12-0	Lecture	Pay.
Saturday	Physical Drill	Internal Economy	----	----

Sutton Veny
10/6/1916.

..................Major,R.A.M.C.(T).
O.C.2/6th London Field Ambulance.

Confidential

War Diary.

of

2/6th London Field Ambulance

from 23rd June 1916 to 30th July 1916.

MEDICAL.

Army Form C. 2118.

WAR DIARY
or
INTELLIGENCE SUMMARY
(Erase heading not required.)

1/6 London Field Ambulance   Sheet 1.

Instructions regarding War Diaries and Intelligence Summaries are contained in F. S. Regs., Part II. and the Staff Manual respectively. Title pages will be prepared in manuscript.

Hour, Date, Place	Summary of Events and Information	Remarks and references to Appendices
23.6.16. 4.20 A.M. WARMINSTER.	Unit entrained for SOUTHAMPTON.	9/15
6.P.M. 23.6.16.1. SOUTHAMPTON.	Unit embarked in 2 parties. Transport, Headquarters and half of personnel in S.S. AUSTRALIND. Remainder on S.S. MONA QUEEN.	9/15
8 A.M. 24.6.16 Le HAVRE.	Both parties disembarked. No casualties during voyage. Unit marched to No 2. REST CAMP. SANVIC.	M/5
4 P.M. 25.6.16.	Unit entrained at GARE DES MARCHANDISES. Two loaves en route during which tea was served and rations issued.	Ports
9 A.M. 26.6.16. St. POL.	Unit detrained, no casualties during journey, marched to billets at NEUVILLE-AU-CORNET.	Ports
9 A.M. 27.6.16 NEUVILLE-AU-CORNET	Seven motor ambulances, 2 motor cycles and 12 personnel attached from 60th DIVISIONAL SUPPLY COLUMN. M.T. Capt SMITH A.B.P. and 10 NCO's and men of C Section attached for duty with 42nd CAS. CLEARING STATION (AUBIGNY) Sergt. GUMBIE G. evacuated sick to No 12 STATIONARY HOSPITAL — (St POL)	Appendix I

Army Form C. 2118.

WAR DIARY
or
INTELLIGENCE SUMMARY
(Erase heading not required.)

2/6 London Field Ambulance
Sheet II

Instructions regarding War Diaries and Intelligence Summaries are contained in F.S. Regs, Part II. and the Staff Manual respectively. Title pages will be prepared in manuscript.

Hour, Date, Place	Summary of Events and Information	Remarks and references to Appendices
12.45 P.M. 27.6.16. NEUVILLE-AU-CORNET	Received orders to proceed to billets at GUESTREVILLE. Water supply bad. Obtained from river 3 kilometres distant.	JWB
28.6.16. GUESTREVILLE. 29.6.16 GUESTREVILLE 30.6.16 GUESTREVILLE	Reception Hospital formed. 5 patients admitted at this place. B section (complete less equipment) attached for instructional purposes to 2/1st HIGHLAND FIELD AMBULANCE	JWB JWB
10.30 A.M. 1.7.16.	Cash obtained from Field Cashier (AUBIGNY) and an issue made to men. Unit proceeded by road to MINGOVAL in accordance with orders from A.D.M.S. 60th LOND DIVN. A billet Hospital was formed. Men were accommodated in huts. Officers in cotts. Horses picketted in the open.	JWB
2.7.16. MINGOVAL. 9 am 3.7.16. 6 pm	Church Parade. Men employed on fatigues. Party consisting of Capt PHILPOT, one Sergeant, one Infant'y officer & 2 Stokers proceeded to CAMBLIGNEUL & take charge of Divisional Baths & also received from ADMS 60 (London) Divison.	

WAR DIARY or INTELLIGENCE SUMMARY

Army Form C. 2118.

2/6 London Field Ambulance
Sheet III

Hour, Date, Place		Summary of Events and Information	Remarks and references to Appendices
MINGOVAL 4.7.16	5pm	Pte Coxhill 10/15 transferred to D.D.M.S Office 17 Corps AUBIGNY.	JNB
5.7.16	9 am	Officers & men of C Section attached to 1/2 Highland Field Ambulance for instruction at ECOIVRES by order of A.D.M.S. 60 (London) Division	JNB
	4 pm	Officers & men of B Section returned to unit from course of instruction at HAUTEVILLERS	
6.7.16	8 pm	2 Horse Ambulance Wagons with drivers reported to M.O. 2/23 Battalion at & on loan by order of A.D.M.S. 60 (London) Division	JNB
7.7.16	am	22513 Pte ROWE W.G. and 2066 Pte BRYCE J.H. officers JNB admitted to 2/6 London Field Ambulance Hospital, been employed in kitchen.	

1247 W 3299 200,000 (E) 8/14 J.B.C. & A. Forms/C. 2118/11.

Army Form C. 2118.

WAR DIARY
or
INTELLIGENCE SUMMARY

(Erase heading not required.)

2/6 London Field Ambulance
Sheet IV.

Instructions regarding War Diaries and Intelligence Summaries are contained in F. S. Regs., Part II. and the Staff Manual respectively. Title pages will be prepared in manuscript.

Hour, Date, Place	Summary of Events and Information	Remarks and references to Appendices
HINGOVAL 8.7.16. pm	2 Coad Economy	pub
9.7.16 pm 10pm	Church Parade. B' ration & daily admin forwarded to Tincques for baths. 1095 S/Sgt MONTAGUE. W.T.) promoted Sergeant 2003 S/M MATTHEWS. P.C.) D.O. 22.6.16. 1092 S/M MEAD. C.A. — 2125 Cpl. LOWRY. R.J. promoted S/Sgt. D.O. 23.1.16. 1911. S/Sgt SCRUTTON W.H. promoted Qm Sergeant. D.O. 23.6.16. 1491. R/m. LEAHY. S.J. next Grade	pub

Army Form C. 2118.

WAR DIARY
or
INTELLIGENCE SUMMARY

2/6 Loram Field Ambulance
Sheet V.

(Erase heading not required.)

Hour, Date, Place	Summary of Events and Information	Remarks and references to Appendices
KINGORSL 10.7.16 9am	Officers & men of 'A' section proceeded to HAUTEN AVENUE for attachment to the 1/6 Highland Field Ambulance for instruction by the 1 A.D.M.S. 61 (2nd) Division. 2043 Cpl BRITTEN. H.V. awarded 20 days Field Punishment No 2 for 'failing to comply with a lawful command given by a Superior Officer'. 2034 Pte NETUPIL.R awarded 10 days Field Punishment No 2. for conduct prejudicial to good order & military discipline.	NB
5pm.	Officers & men of 'C' Section regained unit.	

Army Form C. 2118.

2/6 London Field Ambulance
Sheet VI

WAR DIARY
INTELLIGENCE SUMMARY
(Erase heading not required.)

Instructions regarding War Diaries and Intelligence Summaries are contained in F. S. Regs., Part II. and the Staff Manual respectively. Title pages will be prepared in manuscript.

Hour, Date, Place		Summary of Events and Information	Remarks and references to Appendices
MINGOVAL 12.7.16	9.0 a.m.	Orders received to take over from 2/1st Highland Field Ambulance at HAUTE AVESNES. Advance party under CAPT. MATTHEWS proceeded by March route to HAUTE AVESNES during the morning. The Main Dressing Station, Advanced Dressing Station & Aid Posts were taken over by this party at midnight. 1/3rd Highland Division joined the advance party at HAUTE AVESNES.	MoB Pros
MINGOVAL 13.7.16	9.0 a.m.	Main body left for HAUTE AVESNES, arriving about mid-day. Those men of the advance party who had been on night duty were relieved and duties were organised to form two shifts, mounting at 7.0 a.m. & 7.0 p.m. respectively at	gng
HAUTE AVESNES 13.7.16	12 noon		
HAUTE AVESNES 14.7.16		All general duty men available employed on Pioneer duties, to clean up and tidy the camp as far as possible.	MoB

Army Form C. 2118.

WAR DIARY
or
INTELLIGENCE SUMMARY
(Erase heading not required.)

1/1 Loan Field Ambulance
Sheet VII

Hour, Date, Place	Summary of Events and Information	Remarks and references to Appendices
HAUTE AVESNES 15.7.16 to 18.7.16	Nothing of importance took place except the ordinary work of collecting, remaining sick & wounded from the line &c. At no time were any large	9/18
19.7.16 (& 6.7.16)	Excessive numbers of casualties admitted. Pte. JONES, M.H. attached for duty with No. 16 Kite Balloon Sec. R.F.C. Arrangements made to relieve one half of the men employed at the advanced stations, the relief being carried out with the aid of G.S. wagons.	
20.7.16	The men relieved were absorbed into the day duties left vacant. The second half of the men employed at the advanced stations were relieved.	9/19
21.7.16	S/M. PEARSON, J. evacuated sick to No. 19 Casualty Clearing Station. PTE. CHAMPION, E.G. reported for duty as a reinforcement. A party of reinforcements of infantry, passing camp, were provided with drinking water & hot tea, and minor oak cases attended to.	9/20

WAR DIARY
or
INTELLIGENCE SUMMARY

(Erase heading not required.)

Army Form C. 2118.

2/6 London Field Ambulance

Sheet VIII

Hour, Date, Place	Summary of Events and Information	Remarks and references to Appendices
HAUTE AVESNES 9.0 a.m. 24.7.16. week ending 29.7.16	The G.O.C. 60 (London) Division inspected the field ambulance. During the week further pioneering work was carried out to improve the camp. A separate cookhouse for patients was constructed, the men's cookhouse repaired and a workshop for carpenters erected. One of the Motor Ambulances was covered with expanded metal as a protection against shell fire.	MSS MSS
29.7.16	The Ambulance was inspected by the Director of Medical Services, 3rd Army.	MSS

[signature] Lt Col.
Commanding
2/6th London Field Ambulance.

MEDICAL.

Aug. 1916.

Confidential

War Diary

of

2/6th London Field Ambulance

from 1st August 1916 to 31st August 1916

Vol 3

MEDICAL Army Form C. 2118.

WAR DIARY
or
INTELLIGENCE SUMMARY   2/6th London Field Ambulance.

(Erase heading not required.)

Instructions regarding War Diaries and Intelligence Summaries are contained in F. S. Regs, Part II. and the Staff Manual respectively. Title pages will be prepared in manuscript.

Hour, Date, Place	Summary of Events and Information	Remarks and references to Appendices
1st August 1916 HAUTE AVESNES	All bivouacs used by personnel for sleeping purposes dispensed with, the rough wood & other materials collected and either used for firewood or minor camp improvements.	JMB
2nd August 1916 HAUTE AVESNES	Hostile aeroplanes came over and during the attack by our anti-aircraft guns numerous pieces of shell casing &c fell into the main dressing station. One piece fell through the roof of an operating tent narrowly missing a sergeant. There were no casualties.	JMB
3rd August 1916 HAUTE AVESNES	A water cart sent to the I.O.M. XVII Corps for repair & the water supply rendered difficult to maintain; an adequate supply of chlorinated water two barrels taken into use & conveyed to the pump by limber-wagon.	JMB
4th August 1916 HAUTE AVESNES	Nothing of importance occurred.	JMB

Army Form C. 2118.

2/6th London Field Ambulance

WAR DIARY
or
INTELLIGENCE SUMMARY
(Erase heading not required.)

Hour, Date, Place	Summary of Events and Information	Remarks and references to Appendices
5th Aug. '16 HAUTE AVESNES	COLONEL GRAY, Consulting Surgeon, THIRD ARMY, visited the Field Ambulance. LIEUT L.F. McDOWELL detailed for temporary duty with the 172nd Tunnelling Co. R.E.	9nr13 Appendix 1
6th Aug. '16 HAUTE AVESNES	A shelter erected as a barber's shop for Kavanating under regimental arrangements.	9nr13
7th Aug '16 HAUTE AVESNES	LIEUT L.F. McDOWELL returned.	9nr13
7th to 12th Aug '16 HAUTE AVESNES ANZIN	General pioneer work carried out to improve the condition of the Main Dressing Station Camp. The new Cookhouse rebuilt and a Disinfector shed erected. Further improvements made at the Advanced Dressing Station. An unusually large number of sick men admitted from Field Ambulance personnel.	9nr13

Army Form C. 2118.

WAR DIARY
~~INTELLIGENCE SUMMARY~~
(Erase heading not required.)

2/1st London Field Ambulance

Hour, Date, Place	Summary of Events and Information	Remarks and references to Appendices
11th Aug. 1916 HAUTE AVESNES.	CAPT. J. FIELD HALL and the N.C.O. and 9 men attached to No. 42 CASUALTY CLEARING STN. returned to duty.	JMB
12th & 13th Aug. 1916 HAUTE AVESNES	The establishment of 1st & 2nd Class Orderlies completed by appointments among the personnel of the Unit. A new rubbish pit dug & pla one fitted in. A galvanised iron incinerator erected for burning excreta from the wards.	JMB
14th Aug. 1916 HAUTE AVESNES	Further improvements made in the transport lines and a new covered dust-pit-latrine built for the use of transport personnel.	JMB
15th Aug. 1916 HAUTE AVESNES	2245 PTE C. C. CRAWFURD proceeded to England to Cadet School. (War Office Letter CR No 3312/(1/B)	JMB

Army Form C. 2118.

2/6th London Field Ambulance

WAR DIARY
or
INTELLIGENCE SUMMARY
(Erase heading not required.)

Army Form C. 2118.

Instructions regarding War Diaries and Intelligence Summaries are contained in F. S. Regs., Part II. and the Staff Manual respectively. Title pages will be prepared in manuscript.

Hour, Date, Place	Summary of Events and Information	Remarks and references to Appendices
18th Aug 1916 HAUTE AVESNES	Scottie Cart returned from repair. Fire appliances tested as per G.R.O. 1733.	GNB
19th Aug 1916 HAUTE AVESNES	Capt. G.L. THORNTON detailed for temporary duty as Medical Officer to 1/12th Royal North Lancs. (Pioneer) Battn. 2 men reported as reinforcements. Corpl. PRICE to course of Instruction at tunnel Anti Gas School.	Appendix 2. GNB
18th Aug 1916 HAUTE AVESNES	A fairly large number of sick men were admitted to Hospital. P.U.O being noticeably prevalent.	GNB
LILLE ROAD	A small party proceeded to LILLE ROAD AID POST for road repairing, the work being done between 9.0 p.m. & 2.0 a.m.	
19th Aug 1916 HAUTE AVESNES ANZIN	Capt. R.H. ASTBURY reported for temporary duty for instructional purpose. Part of the sand bag construction at the	GNB

1247 W 3299 200,000 (E) 8/14 J.B.C. & A. Forms/C. 2118/11.

Army Form C. 2118.

2/6th London Field Ambulance

WAR DIARY
INTELLIGENCE SUMMARY
(Erase heading not required.)

Hour, Date, Place	Summary of Events and Information	Remarks and references to Appendices
19th Aug '16 (Contd) LILLE ROAD	Advanced Dressing Station collapsed. A further party proceeded to LILLE ROAD to carry on road repairing.	JWB
20th Aug '16 HAUTE AVESNES	CAPT. J. FIELD HALL proceeded to ROUEN. (G.H.Q. 24/236)	Appendix 3
AUX RIETZ	Orders received from the A.D.M.S. for wounded + sick from the Advanced Dressing Station of the 2/4th London Field Ambulance at AUX RIETZ to be evacuated to the Main Dressing Station of the 2/6th Lon. Field Ambulance from midnight Sunday/Monday to midnight Tues/Wed. of every week.	JWB
	CORPL. FARROW to brune at Divisional Anti-Gas School.	
21st Aug '16 HAUTE AVESNES	A road commenced leading from front to rear of the Main Dressing Station Camp.	JWB

Army Form C. 2118.

WAR DIARY
INTELLIGENCE SUMMARY
(Erase heading not required.)

3/6 London Field Ambulance

Hour, Date, Place	Summary of Events and Information	Remarks and references to Appendices
22nd Aug 1916 HAUTE AVESNES	500 rolls of tarred felt obtained and a party detailed to re-roof the huts.	9NVB
24th Aug 1916 HAUTE AVESNES	Arrangements made for an Officer (attached) 1 NCO & 10 men of the 6/5th London Field Ambulance to take the place of a corresponding number of our personnel at the Advanced Posts. Corpl. PALMER to Bourse at Duni. Ant - Gas School.	NVS
27th Aug 1916 HAUTE AVESNES	One Miller James Stretcher carriage sent to 24th M.A.C. for conversion into 2 wheeled carriages. Three carriages, stretcher, ambulance obtained from Ordnance Dump. A billet taken in the village for R.A.M.C personnel for which no accommodation could be found in the Camp.	9NVB

Army Form C. 2118.

WAR DIARY
INTELLIGENCE SUMMARY 2/6th London Field Ambulance
(Erase heading not required.)

Hour, Date, Place	Summary of Events and Information	Remarks and references to Appendices
28th Aug 1916 HAUTE AVESNES	Orders received from ADMS to send 8 bearers to relieve to R.A.P. POSTE DE LILLE from midnight till morning, also a M.O. to ROUTE DE LILLE Collecting Post for the same period.	Appendix 4 MSB
29th Aug 1916 HAUTE AVESNES	Heavy rain interfered with the work of re-roofing and road construction.	MSB
30th Aug 1916 HAUTE AVESNES	Part of the unused corridor between the Surgical ward & medical ward No.1 converted into a store for reserve medical supplies, linen & clothing	MSB

McBrid Lt Col
.... Commanding
2/6th London Field Ambulance.

WAR DIARY
or
INTELLIGENCE SUMMARY.
(Erase heading not required.)

Army Form C. 2118.

Hour, Date, Place	Summary of Events and Information	Remarks and references to Appendices
SUTTON VENY		
1.6.16 to 3.6.16 6pm	Training as in programme	Appendix "A" attd
4.6.16 to 6.6.16 6pm	Training as in programme	Appendix "B" attd
7.6.16 3pm	Capt. PAVEY-SMITH, Capt. COMYN and Capt. WILLETT reported for duty.	attd
10.6.16 to 13.6.16	Training as in programme	Appendix "C" attd
14.6.16 3pm	Orders received for move tomorrow	attd

Army Form C. 2118.

WAR DIARY
or
INTELLIGENCE SUMMARY.
(Erase heading not required.)

Instructions regarding War Diaries and Intelligence Summaries are contained in F. S. Regs., Part II. and the Staff Manual respectively. Title pages will be prepared in manuscript.

Hour, Date, Place	Summary of Events and Information	Remarks and references to Appendices
SUTTON VENY 16.6.16. to 22.6.16.	Instructions re Division proceeding overseas for the last own leaps carried out.	Appendix "D". seen.

(73989) W4141—463. 400,000. 9/14. H.&J.Ltd. Forms/C. 2118/10.

MEDICAL.

2nd/6th LONDON
29 SEP. 1916
FIELD AMBULANCE

Vol 4

COMMITTEE FOR THE
MEDICAL HISTORY OF THE WAR
Date 26 OCT. 1915

60th Div

Sept 1916

Confidential

War Diary

of

2/6th London Field Ambulance

from 1st September 1916 to 30th September 1916

MEDICAL.

Sheet 1. Army Form C. 2118.

2/6th London Field Ambulance

WAR DIARY
INTELLIGENCE SUMMARY.
(Erase heading not required.)

Hour, Date, Place	Summary of Events and Information	Remarks and references to Appendices
1st. Sept. 1916 HAUTE AVESNES	Between 1.15 & 2.15 pm several shells were fired on the village occupied by the Battalion in rest, 181st Infantry Brigade, causing some casualties. Three motor ambulances and a party of 1 Medical Officer, 2 N.C.O's & 16 men were despatched upon receipt of telephone information to attend to casualties. CAPT. R.H. ASTBURY to 2/22nd Battalion London Regt. as Medical Officer.	JWhd ADMS Letter M.604 dated 30.8.16
3rd. Sept. 1916 HAUTE AVESNES	Upon instructions of A.D.M.S. 60th (London) Division, one Motor Ambulance permanently detailed to be stationed at 18 Ambulance Stores MAROEUIL. Orders received to send 8 bearers & stretchers to Left Battn. Right Sector by midnight. Party left Main Dressing Station at 2.0 pm. CAPT. A.B. PAVER SMITH returned to duty.	ADMS Letter M.785 dated 2.9.16 ADMS Telegram M 797 JWhd
4th Sept. 1916 HAUTE AVESNES.	CAPT. M.V. WILSON detailed for temporary duty as M.O. 60th (London) Divisional Convalescent Camp. Men of Unit billeted in a large hut in HAUTE AVESNES	ADMS Letter M 775 dated 1.9.16. JWhd

Army Form C. 2118.

Sheet 2
2/6th London Field Ambulance

WAR DIARY
or
INTELLIGENCE SUMMARY.
(Erase heading not required.)

Instructions regarding War Diaries and Intelligence Summaries are contained in F.S. Regs., Part II. and the Staff Manual respectively. Title pages will be prepared in manuscript.

Hour, Date, Place	Summary of Events and Information	Remarks and references to Appendices
5th Sept. 1916 HAUTE AVESNES	Rain hampered outdoor pioneer work considerably. The rear portion of the hut used for Reception Room & Park Store, having been dispensed with for sleeping purposes, preparations were made for converting it into an emergency Dressing & Operating Room in case of heavy casualties. A large supply of Dressings & Medical Comforts for 300 wounded issued for use in emergency at the Headquarters of the Battalion in Reserve.	Shepherd
6th – 10th Sept. 1916	Nothing of importance occurred during this period beyond the normal working of the Field Ambulance	Shepherd
11th Sept 1916 HAUTE AVESNES	Two wounded GERMAN prisoners were included among the admissions. CAPT. M.T.G. CLEGG detailed for temporary duty as M.O. 2/3rd Batt. LONDON REGT.	A.D.M.S. Telegram M861 dated 11.9.16 Shepherd

Army Form C. 2118.

Sheet 3
2/6th London Field Ambulance

WAR DIARY
INTELLIGENCE SUMMARY.
(Erase heading not required.)

Instructions regarding War Diaries and Intelligence Summaries are contained in F.S. Regs., Part II. and the Staff Manual respectively. Title pages will be prepared in manuscript.

Hour, Date, Place	Summary of Events and Information	Remarks and references to Appendices
14th Sept 1916 HAUTE AVESNES.	Large Corrugated iron water tank obtained to facilitate supply of chlorinated drinking water	Report
17th Sept 1916. HAUTE AVESNES	CAPT. H.A. PHILPOT detailed for temporary duty as M.O. 2/24 Battn. LONDON REGT.	A.D.M.S. Telegram M912-17-9-16 Further
20th Sept. 1916 HAUTE AVESNES	Orders received from A.D.M.S. 60th (London) Division to send 8 bearers & 4 stretchers to 2/2nd Battn. R.A.P.	ADMS Telegram M.952 d. 20.9.16 further
31st Sept 1916	The G.O.C. 60th (LONDON) DIVISION inspected the MAIN DRESSING STATION. CAPT. M.U. WILSON returned from the 60 DIVN. CONVALESCENT CAMP, his place being taken by CAPT. A.R. COMYN. CAPT. G.L. THORNTON returned from duty with the 1/12 Battn. LOYAL NORTH LANCS. REGT. Orders received to send 8 bearers and 4 stretchers to 2/3rd Battn. R.A.P. for the night.	Report A.D.M.S. Telegram M.960 dated 21/9/16

Army Form C. 2118.

Sheet 17
2/6th London Field Ambulance

WAR DIARY
or
INTELLIGENCE SUMMARY.
(Erase heading not required.)

Instructions regarding War Diaries and Intelligence Summaries are contained in F.S. Regs., Part II. and the Staff Manual respectively. Title pages will be prepared in manuscript.

Hour, Date, Place	Summary of Events and Information	Remarks and references to Appendices
22nd Sept. 1916 ANZIN. HAUTE AVESNES	THE DIRECTOR OF MEDICAL SERVICES, FIRST ARMY inspected the ADVANCED DRESSING STATION and the MAIN DRESSING STATION.	Jethral
23rd Sept. 1916 HAUTE AVESNES	Orders received from the A.D.M.S. 60th (London) Division to send Stretcher Bearers to the 2/21st Battn. R.A.P. also a M.O. to LILLE ROAD COLLECTING POST.	Jethral
25th Sept. 1916 HAUTE AVESNES	The Transport Lines were removed from another situation and preparations made for the construction of winter standings.	Jethral
28th Sept. 1916 HAUTE AVESNES	A supply of gravel obtained and construction of winter standings for Motor Ambulances commenced.	M.S.

(73989) W4141—463. 400,000. 9/14. H.&J. Ltd. Forms/C. 2118/10.

Capt Dew

2/6 London Y. Amb.

Col rath

COMMITTEE FOR THE
MEDICAL HISTORY OF THE WAR
Date -2 DEC. 1916

Confidential

War Diary

of the

2/6 London Field Ambulance

From October 1st 1916 To October 31st 1916

WAR DIARY
— or —
INTELLIGENCE SUMMARY.

(Erase heading not required.)

2/6th London Field Ambulance
Sheet 1.

Army Form C. 2118.

Hour, Date, Place	Summary of Events and Information	Remarks and references to Appendices
1st Oct. 1916 HAUTE AVESNES	LIEUT. ATKINSON reported for temporary duty and instruction. He was detailed for duty at the ADVANCED DRESSING STATION.	PWS.
3rd Oct. 1916 HAUTE AVESNES	5 men detached for duty at DIVISIONAL BATHS. 8 men & 4 stretchers to L. Battn. Right Sector to assist with any extra casualties arising from a Raid.	PWS
4th Oct. 1916 HAUTE AVESNES	CAPT. C.M. KEILLOR reported for temporary duty and instruction.	PWS
5th Oct. 1916 HAUTE AVESNES	5 more men detached for duty at DIVISIONAL BATHS.	PWS
7th Oct. 1916 HAUTE AVESNES	CAPT. KEILLOR detailed for temporary duty as M.O. 60th (London) Divisional Train A.S.C.	PWS
8th Oct 1916 HAUTE AVESNES	8 men & 4 stretchers sent for overnight to Right Battn. Right Sector to deal with any additional casualties resulting from a raid.	PWS

Army Form C. 2118.

2/4th London Field Amb*
Sheet 2

WAR DIARY
INTELLIGENCE SUMMARY
(Erase heading not required.)

Instructions regarding War Diaries and Intelligence Summaries are contained in F.S. Regs., Part II and the Staff Manual respectively. Title pages will be prepared in manuscript.

Hour, Date, Place	Summary of Events and Information	Remarks and references to Appendices
11th Oct. 1916 HAUTE AVESNES	LIEUT. COLONEL BIRD proceeded on leave. – LIEUT. ATKINSON proceeded to join 8th Division. CAPT. THORNTON detailed for temporary duty as M.O. 2/23rd Battn. LONDON REGIMENT in place of CAPT. BELL who reported for temporary duty with the Field Ambulance.	Nil.
14th Oct. 1916 HAUTE AVESNES	Transport inspected by O.C. 520th (1st T.) Co. A.S.C. 12 men and 6 stretchers sent to 2/23rd BATTN. LONDON REGT. to deal with any increased casualties resulting from a raid.	Nil.
18th Oct. 1916 HAUTE AVESNES	LIEUT. COLONEL J.W. BIRD returned from leave. CAPT. BELL returned to 2/23rd BATTN. LONDON REGT., and CAPT. THORNTON returned to duty with the Field Ambulance.	Nil.
21st Oct. 1916 HAUTE AVESNES	An advance party from the 8th CANADIAN FIELD AMBULANCE, consisting of 1 Officer + 8 O.R.s	Nil.

Army Form C. 2118.

2/6th London Field Ambulance
Sheet - 3

WAR DIARY
INTELLIGENCE SUMMARY.
(Erase heading not required.)

Hour, Date, Place	Summary of Events and Information	Remarks and references to Appendices
21st Oct. 1916 (contd.) HAUTE AVESNES	reported for the purpose of learning the routes in the trenches etc. 2 clerks reported later.	9w3.
23rd Oct 1916 HAUTE AVESNES ANZIN	The main body of the 8th CANADIAN FIELD AMBULANCE arrived at 12.0 Noon. 1 Section was sent up to the ADVANCED DRESSING STATION, and upon relief by them the personnel of the 2/6th LONDON FIELD AMBULANCE marched back to the MAIN DRESSING STATION, bringing all wheeled stretcher carriages.	9w3
HAUTE AVESNES	The MAIN DRESSING STATION was handed over at 6.0 p.m. The personnel of this unit however remained in its billets until the next morning.	

Army Form C. 2118.

26th London Field Amb[ulance]
Sheet 4

WAR DIARY
INTELLIGENCE SUMMARY.
(Erase heading not required.)

Hour, Date, Place	Summary of Events and Information	Remarks and references to Appendices
24th Oct 1916. HAUTE AVESNES	The Unit proceeded at 7.30 a.m. by march route to IVERGNY but en route information was received that billeting area was changed to SUS-ST-LEGER. The weather was very unfavorable. All troops were billeted by 4.30 p.m.	MWS
SUS-ST-LEGER.	A RECEPTION HOSPITAL was opened, evacuations being made to No.6 STA. HOSPL. FREVENT.	
25th Oct 1916 SUS-ST-LEGER	A balloon was found to have descended in the vicinity of the billets and a party was detailed to fold it up & transmit the weather continues to the extremely bad.	MWS
25th Oct 1916 SUS-ST-LEGER	The Unit proceeded by march route at 9.0 a.m. to NEUVILLETTE, arriving at 12.30 p.m. A RECEPTION HOSPITAL was opened.	MWS

Army Form C. 2118.

WAR DIARY
or
INTELLIGENCE SUMMARY.

2/1st London Field Ambulance Sheet 5

(Erase heading not required.)

Hour, Date, Place	Summary of Events and Information	Remarks and references to Appendices
29th Oct 1916. NEUVILLETTE MON PLAISIR.	The unit proceeded by march route to MONTPLAISIR, leaving at 7.15am marching with the 181st Infantry Brigade. Sick patch upon the line ground were evacuated to No. 19 Casualty Clearing Station.	JHS.
30th Oct 1916 MON PLAISIR	The unit still remained at MONTPLAISIR.	JHS.

J.H.Smith.
Lt Colonel.
Comm

Nov. 1916

CONFIDENTIAL

WAR DIARY

of

2/6th London Field Ambulance — 60th (London) Division.

from November 1st 1916 to November 30th 1916.

[stamp: COMMITTEE FOR THE MEDICAL HISTORY OF THE WAR Date 30 APR. 1917]

[stamp: 2/6th LONDON FIELD AMBULANCE]

J. M. Bird
Lt. Colonel Commanding,
2/6th London Field Ambulance.

Army Form C. 2118.

2/8th London Field Ambulance
Sheet 1.

WAR DIARY
INTELLIGENCE SUMMARY.
(Erase heading not required.)

Instructions regarding War Diaries and Intelligence Summaries are contained in F.S. Regs., Part II. and the Staff Manual respectively. Title pages will be prepared in manuscript.

Hour, Date, Place	Summary of Events and Information	Remarks and references to Appendices
1 Nov 1916 MON PLAISIR.	The Unit went for route march in the morning. At 6.50 pm orders were received to parade the unit ready to move off, on a practice alarm. The unit paraded within 50 minutes (i.e. at 7.40 pm) and was dismissed. The weather during the day was fair in the morning, wet after noon.	Noted
2. Nov. 1916 NON PLAISIR.	Capt. KEILLOR detailed for duty with the 2/21st Battn. LONDON REGT. & struck off strength. Capt. CLEGG returned to the Unit from the 2/21st Battn. LONDON REGT. The personnel of the Unit was inspected by the A.D.M.S. 60th (LONDON) DIVISION.	Noted
3 Nov 1916 MON PLAISIR. — GORGES.	The Unit proceeded by march route to GORGES starting at 9.0 am and arriving about mid-day. Billeting accommodation fairly satisfactory.	Noted
4 Nov 1916 GORGES. — VAUCHELLES-LES- DO.MART.	The Unit proceeded by march route to VAUCHELLES-LES-DOMART starting at 9.0 am and arriving at 1.0 pm (appox). Billets were secured. A Reception Hospital was formed.	Noted

Army Form C. 2118.

2/6 London Field Ambulance
Sheet 2.

WAR DIARY
INTELLIGENCE SUMMARY.
(Erase heading not required.)

Instructions regarding War Diaries and Intelligence Summaries are contained in F.S. Regs., Part II and the Staff Manual respectively. Title pages will be prepared in manuscript.

Hour, Date, Place	Summary of Events and Information	Remarks and references to Appendices
6 Nov. 1916 VAUCHELLES-LES-DOMART	4 Limbered G.S. wagons & 6 L.D. Horses handed over to No 4 Coy. 60th Div Train	posted.
8 Nov 1916 VAUCHELLES-L-DOMI.	Capt. WILSON detailed for temporary duty as M.O. 2/12th Battn London Regt. 2 Officers & 5 O.Rs allowed to proceed to England on leave	posted
10th Nov 1916 VAUCHELLES-L-DOMI.	8 L.D. Horses exchanged for mules	posted
11. Nov. 1916 VAUCHELLES-L-DOMI.	The 6 motor Ambulances & 2 motor bicycles attached were sent to 60 Div Supply Column. Another Motor Ambulance reported for duty. 36 Mules were received. — LIEUT. L.F. McDOWELL transferred to 33RD DIVISION. — LIEUT. R. GOVAN reported for duty	posted
12 Nov. 1916	Capt. COMYN transferred to C.R.E. 60th DIVN — Capt. THORNTON transferred to 60 1st Div AMMN. COLUMN. 2 R & R.O reported as reinforcements. Capt. C.H. NEWTON & Capt. A.R. ESLER reported for duty.	posted

(73989) W.4141—463. 400,000. 9/14. H.&J.Ltd. Forms/C. 2118/10.

Army Form C. 2118.

2/6th London Field Ambulance
Sheet 3

WAR DIARY
INTELLIGENCE SUMMARY.
(Erase heading not required.)

Instructions regarding War Diaries and Intelligence Summaries are contained in F.S. Regs, Part II and the Staff Manual respectively. Title pages will be prepared in manuscript.

Hour, Date, Place	Summary of Events and Information	Remarks and references to Appendices
13 NOV. 1916. VAUCHELLES-L-DOM.T.	50 A.S.C. reinforcements arrived. The iron ration in possession of the personnel of the Unit were commuted by order of the G.O.C. 60th Divn., as part of the dump ration. LIEUT. S. NIX reported for duty	Initial.
14 NOV. 1916. VAUCHELLES-L-DOM.T.	1 Motor Ambulance reported for temporary duty. 4 O.R.'s R.A.M.C. reported as reinforcements. 1 Maltese Cart was handed over to H.Q. Co. 60th DIV. TRAIN.	Initial.
15 NOV. 1916. VAUCHELLES-L-DOM.T.	1 more Motor Ambulance reported for temporary duty	Initial.
16 NOV. 1916. VAUCHELLES-L-DOM.T. (BELLANCOURT)	105 A.S.C. reinforcements were received but were billetted at BELLACOURT through lack of accommodation.	Initial.
17 NOV. 1916.	5 O.R.'s R.A.M.C. arrived as reinforcements; making R.A.M.C. personnel above establishment. Capt. NEWTON transferred to 2/5th LONDON FIELD AMBULANCE.	Initial.

Army Form C. 2118.

2/6th London Field Ambulance
Sheet 4

WAR DIARY
INTELLIGENCE SUMMARY.
(Erase heading not required.)

Instructions regarding War Diaries and Intelligence Summaries are contained in F.S. Regs., Part II. and the Staff Manual respectively. Title pages will be prepared in manuscript.

Hour, Date, Place	Summary of Events and Information	Remarks and references to Appendices
18 Nov. 1916 VAUCHELLES-L-DOMT	LIEUT. S. NIX transferred to 2/23rd Batt. LONDON REGT. as M.O. The 105 A.S.C. reinforcements moved from BEAUCOURT and billeted in VAUCHELLES-L-DOMART and BRUCAMPS.	Fine
19 Nov. 1916 VAUCHELLES-L-DOMT	1 Motor Ambulance returned to A.D.M.S. office. CAPT. ESLER transferred to 4th Divn. CAPT. D. POTTINGER (M.C.) and CAPT. E.P. BLASHKI reported for duty.	Fine
23 Nov. 1916 VAUCHELLES-L-DOMT	All remaining G.S. Wagons & Heavy Ambulance Wagons, together with Heavy draught Horses, handed in to Base H.T. Depot ABBEVILLE. Reception doubtful. Close.	Fine
24 Nov. 1916 VAUCHELLES-L-DOMT	Unit entrained at LONGPRE for MARSEILLES. The journey was made in two parties. Equipment conveyed in motor lorries.	Fine
27 Nov. 1916 MARSEILLES	Unit detrained at MARSEILLES in the early morning and marched to Rest Camp, where transport & enough personnel to look after the horses and mules going on were LA VALENTINE and the remainder marched to Camp MUSSOT. The Unit remainder have until the 3rd Dec.	Fine

www.ingramcontent.com/pod-product-compliance
Lightning Source LLC
Chambersburg PA
CBHW081431160426
43193CB00013B/2245